Educational Communications and Technology: Issues and Innovations

Series editors

J. Michael Spector
M.J. Bishop
Dirk Ifenthaler

More information about this series at http://www.springer.com/series/11824

Demetria Loryn Ennis-Cole

Technology for Learners with Autism Spectrum Disorders

Springer

Demetria Loryn Ennis-Cole
Department of Learning Technologies
University of North Texas
   Discovery Park
Denton, TX
USA

ISBN 978-3-319-05980-8   ISBN 978-3-319-05981-5 (eBook)
DOI 10.1007/978-3-319-05981-5

Library of Congress Control Number: 2014945806

Springer Cham Heidelberg New York Dordrecht London

© Springer International Publishing Switzerland 2015
This work is subject to copyright. All rights are reserved by the Publisher, whether the whole or part of the material is concerned, specifically the rights of translation, reprinting, reuse of illustrations, recitation, broadcasting, reproduction on microfilms or in any other physical way, and transmission or information storage and retrieval, electronic adaptation, computer software, or by similar or dissimilar methodology now known or hereafter developed. Exempted from this legal reservation are brief excerpts in connection with reviews or scholarly analysis or material supplied specifically for the purpose of being entered and executed on a computer system, for exclusive use by the purchaser of the work. Duplication of this publication or parts thereof is permitted only under the provisions of the Copyright Law of the Publisher's location, in its current version, and permission for use must always be obtained from Springer. Permissions for use may be obtained through RightsLink at the Copyright Clearance Center. Violations are liable to prosecution under the respective Copyright Law.
The use of general descriptive names, registered names, trademarks, service marks, etc. in this publication does not imply, even in the absence of a specific statement, that such names are exempt from the relevant protective laws and regulations and therefore free for general use.
While the advice and information in this book are believed to be true and accurate at the date of publication, neither the authors nor the editors nor the publisher can accept any legal responsibility for any errors or omissions that may be made. The publisher makes no warranty, express or implied, with respect to the material contained herein.

Printed on acid-free paper

Springer is part of Springer Science+Business Media (www.springer.com)

Foreword

The book by Dr. Ennis-Cole is an important addition to available resources on teaching students with Autism Spectrum Disorders (ASD). It addresses an area of intervention that has become increasingly popular and widely utilized-technological resources for individuals with autism. Anyone who works in the field of ASD has witnessed the IPAD revolution. The use of the IPAD for people on the spectrum has catapulted. While such movements are exciting and inspiring, they also point out the gaps in our scientific understanding. While the enthusiasm for the use of technology has been high, clinical guidelines have been lacking. Furthermore, little research has been done to identify best applications, effective components, training systems, and the evaluation of impact. Hence, it is an area of great potential utility in need of more research and more description of its applications. The author is to be commended for creating a resource for educators on technology and autism. It is an area where we are all likely to see more growth as the years go by.

It is nice to have so many interventions described in one resource. Every family member and educator who works with people with ASD utilizes many of the strategies on a daily basis—visual cues, video modeling, and augmentative communication devices. Yet how do we utilize them? How do we decide which ones make the most sense for this learner? What do we know about AAC devices, about transitioning students to such devices? What do we know about how to best introduce and expand the functional uses of the IPAD?

The author does an excellent job in the first chapter outlining the theories about autism that describe the central deficits, and she explains how the core triad of symptoms (social and communication deficits and behavioral characteristics) creates educational challenges. Her summary of issues in learning supports a closer examination of how technology might mitigate these challenges.

The Chapter on Technology-Created Visual Support (Chap. 4) is especially helpful for its examples of actual resources that could be used to supplement intervention. It can be challenging to figure out ways to use visual strategies, particularly for academic subject areas such as math and science. The samples used highlight potential uses in multiple ways.

Chapter 5 (Technologies to Facilitate Communication, Social Skill Development, Diagnostic Reporting, and Learning) has several intriguing new directions that may not be familiar to interventionists, and that should be interesting to see evolve. In particular, the use of robotics and video games to teach skills is thought provoking.

It is important for the reader to concentrate on the technologies that have the best data to support their use. Examples include video modeling and a wide variety of visual cues. The author ends the chapter by saying, "At this point in time, computerized tools are not an intervention for ASD, but they are an aid that can provide the engagement and support that helps learners with ASD scaffold content in the areas of communication, social skill development, and behaviour". This is an excellent description of the state of the science regarding the use of such strategies.

A book such as this delineates interventions with some merit or potential merit, and encourages parents and educational team members to explore their utility for individual learners with ASD. The author contextualizes the nature of autism and its impact on every area of life very accurately. She summarizes available literature and identifies procedures that may benefit individuals with ASD. A strong argument is made for understanding the nature of autism and the learning characteristics of learners with autism. This is important, because effective intervention requires an understanding of the challenges individuals with autism face and the accommodations that may make learning more successful and efficient. It is likely that we will see more resources like this in the years to come. This book serves as a compelling call to action. It outlines the potential of technology to make our educational interventions with learners on the autism spectrum more successful. It highlights several well-established interventions (e.g., video modeling) and suggests the potential impact of newer innovations (e.g., robotics). As technology is a moving target, it is hard to imagine how a revision of this book will look years down the road, but it is exciting to imagine!

Melmark   Mary Jane Weiss

Preface

This book was written to share information on the ways technology tools can be used to structure academic content, facilitate visual information processing, and support children with Autism Spectrum Disorder (ASD). As I worked with my son and other children with ASD, I noticed that all of the children were interested in technology tools, and each child had preferences for certain tools and programs. I wanted to explore these areas to better understand the technology-using behaviors of the children. While I worked with children in the Technology and Applied Research in Autism (TARA) Lab, parents shared their insight on the appeal of technology, how their children used their favorite tools, and the educational challenges they faced in school settings. I began interviewing parents to find out more about how they were using technology and how it was used in the schools their children attended. I discovered that most of the children were not using technology a great deal in school. As I thought more about this, I embarked on this project to explain some of the technologies and the ways they could be applied in home and school settings. In this book, I explain some of the dominant theories in ASD, characteristics of learners with ASD, and technologies that may be of assistance. Realistic examples, comments from parents, worksheet examples, a list of resources, and tips for working with learners with ASD are interspersed throughout the book to help readers understand the needs of students living with the challenges of ASD.

Demetria Loryn Ennis-Cole

Acknowledgments

I would like to acknowledge all the parents of children who have participated in the Technology and Applied Research in Autism Laboratory and the parents who have shared their stories with me through interviews and surveys on the Internet. They allowed me to enter their world, listen to and read their perspectives, and engage with their children. We logged hundreds of hours together trying to find pieces of the puzzle (Autism); this work is dedicated to them, their courage, and the unwavering love and support they give their children each day.

I would like to acknowledge Ms. Amanda Dailey, who created the artwork that appears in Chap. 4. Ms. Dailey is a senior in Interior Design in the College of Visual Arts and Design at the University of North Texas.

I wish to acknowledge my husband, Melvin Cole, my son with ASD, Miles Cole, my parents, Mr. and Mr. Willie Ennis, Jr., and my mother-in-law, Mrs. Ruby Cole for their inspiration and their faith in my ability to complete this project. It is our combined hope that the information presented will help parents, teachers, therapists, and other individuals who work with children in the Autism Spectrum. We hope this compilation makes providers and carers more patience with individuals with ASD and more willing to explore technologies that can be incorporated into their academic, work, and leisure activities.

Contents

1 **Autism Spectrum Disorders (ASD) and Technology** 1
   1.1 Introduction 1
       1.1.1 Dominant Theories in ASD 3
       1.1.2 Theory of Mind 3
       1.1.3 Executive Dysfunction 4
       1.1.4 Weak Central Coherence 5
   1.2 Characteristics of Individuals with ASD 6
       1.2.1 Perseveration 6
       1.2.2 Sensory Challenges and Motor Skills 7
       1.2.3 Expressive, Receptive, and Pragmatic Language
             Challenges 8
       1.2.4 Social Skills Deficits 9
       1.2.5 Problems with Working Memory 9
       1.2.6 Linear Execution 10
       1.2.7 Stereotypical Behavior 11
       1.2.8 Lack of Academic Motivation 11
       1.2.9 Problems with Reading Comprehension 12
   1.3 Technology and ASD 13
   1.4 Summary 13
   1.5 Discussion Points 13

2 **Strategies for Supporting Students with ASD** 15
   2.1 Introduction 15
       2.1.1 Understanding ASD 15
       2.1.2 Perfectionist Tendencies 16
       2.1.3 Self-stimulatory Behavior 16
       2.1.4 Delayed Echolalia 17
       2.1.5 Meltdowns and Their Meaning 18
       2.1.6 Facilitating Positive Social Interaction 19
       2.1.7 Securing Compliance 20

2.2		Getting Qualified Support	21
	2.2.1	Voting People off the Island	22
	2.2.2	Sensory Issues	22
	2.2.3	Using Direct Language	22
	2.2.4	Using Positive Reinforcement	23
	2.2.5	Gaining the Learner's Attention	23
	2.2.6	Understanding the Theories that Attempt to Explain ASD	23
	2.2.7	Learning to Handle Non-preferred Activities	24
2.3		Applications of Technology	25
2.4		Summary	27
2.5		Discussion Points	27

3 Family Issues in ASD ... 29
3.1		Introduction	29
	3.1.1	Increased Stress	29
	3.1.2	Educational Challenges	31
	3.1.3	The Future	34
	3.1.4	Sibling Issues	35
	3.1.5	Parental Involvement in Educational and Therapy Programs	35
	3.1.6	Behavior of the Child with ASD	36
3.2		Use of Technology	37
3.3		Summary	39
3.4		Discussions Points	39

4 Technology-Created Visual Support ... 41
4.1		Introduction	41
	4.1.1	Examples of Worksheets Created with Applications Software for Learners with ASD	42
	4.1.2	Summary	58
	4.1.3	Discussion Points	58

5 Technologies to Facilitate Communication, Social Skill Development, Diagnostic Reporting, and Learning ... 59
5.1		Introduction	59
	5.1.1	Applications of Video-Modeling	62
5.2		Augmentative and Alternative Communication	65
5.3		Robotics	67
5.4		Virtual Reality	69
5.5		Telepractice/Teletherapy	70
5.6		Video Games	71
5.7		Summary	71
5.8		Discussion Points	72

6	**The Need for Support, Learning Environments,**		
	and Technology Use...		73
	6.1	Introduction	73
		6.1.1 Problems in ASD that Require Support	73
	6.2	Learning Environments in ASD............................	76
	6.3	The Use of Technologies in ASD..........................	78
	6.4	Summary	79
	6.5	Discussion Points..	79

Appendix A: Practical Tips for Assisting Learners with ASD 81

Appendix B: Chapter Resources 85

References 89

Index.. 99

About the Author

Demetria Loryn Ennis-Cole is an Associate Professor in the Department of Learning Technologies at the University of North Texas. She has degrees in Computer Science and Curriculum and Instruction (emphasis area: Computer Education). She worked in industry as a Programmer for International Business Machines and spent 6 years at Louisiana State University as a Computer Analyst before she accepted a faculty position with The University of North Texas. She is a member of several state, national, and international organizations including The Association for Supervision and Curriculum Development, and The International Society for Technology in Education. Her research interest focuses on Technology Utilization by Special Populations (Mature Adults, Children in the Primary Grades, and Children in the Autism Spectrum). She is the director of the Technology and Applied Research in Autism Laboratory (http://tara.unt.edu) for young children in the Autism Spectrum.

Chapter 1
Autism Spectrum Disorders (ASD) and Technology

Theories of ASD, Characteristics of Individuals with ASD and Technology Tools

1.1 Introduction

In 1911 a Swiss psychiatrist named Paul Eugen Bleuler used the term autism to describe symptoms of schizophrenia in mentally ill adults (Autism Epicenter 2008–2011). The Greek word for autism comes from two words—autos and ismos which mean "self-absorbed." Individuals with Autism Spectrum Disorder (ASD) can be absorbed in fascinations and passions in which they intently engage to the exclusion of other activities or interaction with others (Calhoun 2006). In 1943 Leo Kanner coined the term 'infantile autism' in a paper he wrote to describe 11 children with similar characteristics: unusual interests, difficulty interacting, and difficulty communicating (The Alan Mason Chesney Medical Archives of the John Hopkins Medical Institutions 2009). In 1944, Hans Asperger used the phrase 'autistic psychopathy' to describe children with exceptional abilities who were autistic (Ennis-Cole et al. 2013). There are no medical tests or physical markers to determine whether or not a person has ASD (Bregman 2005; Kumar et al. 2010); instead, behavioral observations are used to determine whether or not an individual is in the spectrum.

Several screening instruments are available for identifying ASD in young children: Checklist of Autism in Toddlers (CHAT) and a modified version (M-CHAT), the Screening Tool for Autism in Two-Year-Olds (STAT), the Social Communication Questionnaire (SCQ) for children 4 and older, and the Autism Diagnostic Observation Schedule (ADOS) which can be used for toddlers through adults. The ADOS (Autism Diagnostic Observation Scale created in 1981 by Catherine Lord, Michael Rutter, Pamela DiLoavore, and Susan Risi) and the ADI-R (Autism Diagnostic Interview-Revised created in 2003 for planning treatment and distinguishing ASD from other disorders by Michael Rutter, Ann LeCouter and Catherine Lord) are considered gold-standard assessments for evaluating ASD (South et al. 2007). Tip 1: Get an evaluation from professionals who are using the ADOS and ADI-R.

Other diagnostic tools include The Gilliam Autism Rating Scale and The Childhood Autism Rating Scale. Teams of professionals analyze screening and assessment tools in conjunction with parental questionnaires, developmental histories, results of psychological and intelligence tests, and language assessments to determine severity. ASD leaves no visible signs, but it affects an individual's ability to fully comprehend and use language, interact with others, and behave in socially acceptable ways (Durand 2005; Myles and Simpson 2002; Portway and Johnson 2005). Another screening instrument for determining whether or not an individual has ASD is the Autism Spectrum Quotient, a questionnaire developed by Baron-Cohen et al. (2001). The Autism Spectrum Quotient can be used by both adults and children.

ASD is a costly, life-long disability that affects more males than females. At the present time, the cause is unknown; researchers are examining genetic, biomedical and environmental factors in an effort to determine the cause(s). Several theories have been examined: environmental toxins, vaccines, viruses the mother experienced prenatally and during pregnancy, birth trauma, illnesses, genetics, lack of nurturing by the mother, and others. Two of these have resulted in controversy: a lack of maternal nurturing and vaccines. Leo Kanner coined the phrase 'refrigerator mother' to describe a cold and aloof mother who withheld affection from her child. The mother's lack of affection and emotional bonding with the child was thought to be the cause of ASD. This theory has been refuted (Schreibman 2005). The other controversial theory surrounding the cause of ASD is vaccines. Many parents reported that their children were lethargic, unresponsive, and lost skills they had previously gained after receiving doses of vaccines. Those reports were examined, but empirical studies have failed to link the development of ASD with thimerosal—a mercury containing neurotoxin used to extend the shelf-life of vaccines (CDC 2010). The American Academy of Pediatrics and the Center for Disease Control found high levels of mercury in vaccines and requested the removal of thimerosal as a precautionary measure (CDC 2010; Offit 2007; Parker et al. 2004).

ASD has many variations, and it may likely be caused by a genetic predisposition triggered by various environmental factors. Whatever the cause(s), there are several theories that attempt to explain ASD: Enactive Mind, Mirror Neurons, Systemizing/Empathizing, Theory of Mind, Executive Dysfunction, and Weak Central Coherence A brief discussion of the most dominant theories is presented below. For an in-depth discussion of the theories, examine the works of Baron-Cohen, Frith, Happé, Pellicano, Ozonoff, and others. The discussions below are intended to provide a brief overview, provide practical solutions for overcoming deficits, and discuss technology applications of technology that may provide additional support. Many forms of technology are being included in intervention programs, and more research is needed on the effectiveness of these tools. Families and therapists should be aware that technology tools are an emerging practice, and they should consult The National Autism Center's report on Evidence-Based Interventions (EBI) http://www.nationalautismcenter.org/pdf/NAC%20Standards%20Report.pdf for information on intervention selection and planning. Individuals with ASD have specific characteristics that affect their ability to learn, communicate, and interact with others, and technology can be a useful tool for supporting daily functions, providing instruction, and helping the individual overcome challenges.

1.1.1 Dominant Theories in ASD

Several theories have been proposed to explain ASD: Theory of Mind, Executive Dysfunction and Weak Central Coherence are the older and more dominant explanations in the literature. These theories are not mutually exclusive, and they lead to the creation of new knowledge. Early research highlighted problems with attention, auditory memory, verbal memory, and language (Mann and Walker 2003; Hermelin and O'Connor 1967). In the 1980s, Theory of Mind emerged, and it explained some of the social and communication challenges in ASD (impaired facial recognition, limited imitation, inability to attend to social queues) and postulated that those might stem from a major cognitive deficit (Rajendran and Mitchell 2007). Some researchers noticed that symptoms of ASD were not completely explained by Theory of Mind, but were similar to symptoms of individuals who had frontal lobe injuries: need for sameness, perseveration, lack of impulse control, and difficulty switching attention. This observation led to the Theory of Executive Dysfunction which explained the lack of coping skills demonstrated in daily life by individuals with ASD as well as their difficulties with tasks that required planning and organizing. Executive functions cover a range of high-order control processes for tasks that are not routine: planning, monitoring, generating and manipulating ideas, controlling processes and demonstrating flexibility. The Theory of Weak Central Coherence was proposed to explain the attention to detail demonstrated by individuals with ASD who have the ability to focus on narrow interests and process finite details at the expense of the Gestalt or the global whole. They are exceptional at attending to details, but the integration of details into a larger context is absent. Weak Central Coherence explains problems in information processing, but it also explains superior skills in perceptual discrimination, rote memory, and visuo-spatial performance. Individuals with ASD perform very well on block design tasks and embedded figures tests (Pellicano et al. 2006; Samson et al. 2011; Shah and Frith 1993; Stevenson and Gernsbacher 2013).

1.1.2 Theory of Mind

Many children with ASD have trouble understanding the perspective of another person. What another person thinks and feels eludes them, and often, they need concrete information to understand what others experience, think, or feel. Baron-Cohen (1995, 2008) used Theory of Mind (ToM) to explain a mind blindness which kept a person with ASD from being able to relate to another person's state of mind, feelings, and perception of a situation or event. The term comes from the work of Premack and Woodruff (1978), which describes the ability to impute mental states to others and oneself. An individual with ASD may not understand facial expressions, sense the discomfort of others, or demonstrate empathy. He or she lacks ToM because he or she is unable to understand that others have different thoughts, feelings, beliefs, wants, ideas, and knowledge from themselves. Researchers feel that deficits in this area prevent understanding, interacting, and communicating with others in a purposeful and meaningful way (Baron-Cohen 1995, 2008). Baron-Cohen first described ToM as a deficit in the ability to mentalize; he later modified his theory by saying that a problem with ToM was a delay rather than a deficit. Some researchers found that some individuals with ASD passed the false beliefs tests which were initially used to detect ToM, so advanced tests were developed. Results have been diverse and they have created additional avenues for research. According to Rajendran and Mitchell (2007), ToM and belief attribution studies are waning in both typical and atypical populations, and debates and additional research studies have led to the Enactive Mind Hypothesis. Enactive Mind explains cognition as constructs embedded in experiences that come from a body's action and interaction with important aspects of the environment. It proposes that the process of learning about the world and transferring that knowledge to social action is short circuited in ASD, because typically important social stimuli is absent. Because of this absence, physical stimuli based on the child's selective attention lead the child to focus more on things than people. In Enactive Mind, constructs and definitions are present, but there are no experiences that form the foundation for using and applying the constructs. The absence of embodied social cognitive tools prevents the individual with ASD from producing socially adaptive reactions in natural settings (Klin et al. 2003).

Explicit instruction in feelings and emotions, social skills games, and group interaction (social skills groups) may help the learner with ASD explore ideas and concepts from a different vantage point. Role playing and videos combined with explanations may also help the learner begin to notice differences in people and begin to understand the feelings and emotions of others in relationship to their own. Apps like *The Emotion Detective*, and computer software like *Mind Reading* may also provide opportunities to practice examining facial expressions, emotions, and match those with the appropriate mental states. Various CD products like the *Transporters* and programs like *FaceLand* (http://Do2Learn.com) are also options for providing practice to students who need additional help recognizing facial expressions and emotions.

1.1.3 Executive Dysfunction

Executive Dysfunction has been used to explain some of the rigidity in ASD (Frith 2001; Calhoun 2006; White 2013), including repetitive behaviors, restrictive interests, and socio-communicative difficulties. There are many definitions of executive function, and there are inconsistencies and complexities. Researchers cannot create tests that measure only one aspect of executive function, because of its multifaceted nature. There is also debate on the relationship between executive processes and ToM, the intricate relationship between executive function and language, and the best strategies for developing and remediating deficits in this area.

1.1 Introduction

Many researchers across different fields (e.g., cognitive science, neuropsychology, neurology, education, etc.) are involved in examining this important area of human function. Calhoun (2006) indicates that the literature broadly defines executive function as a cognitive skill which orchestrates tasks that depend on goal-attainment and self-regulation. A more precisely defined set of cognitive domains emerges from research on executive function. It is generally agreed that the following components are affected: inhibition, cognitive flexibility/shifting, working memory, generality, self-monitoring, and planning (Calhoun 2006; Hill 2004; White 2013). Deficits in executive function can be observed when an individual with ASD is unable to switch from one mode of thinking to another. It is also present when a person continues with an argument when given direct feedback that the argument is incorrect (South et al. 2007). Some intervention strategies include teaching delayed responding, providing organizational support, and self-talk. Organizational support can be provided electronically in the form of electronic reminders via email and tablet computers, visual schedules that are computerized or printed manually, flow diagrams, and charting. Charting will be discussed in Chap. 4 as an instructional strategy, and many examples will be presented in different content areas describing the ways charts can be used to chunk important concepts, provide a visual reference, make spelling words easier to understand, serve as an advanced organizer, strengthen computational skills, provide a review, and promote retention.

1.1.4 Weak Central Coherence

Weak Central Coherence explains some of the social and anti-social behaviour in ASD, as well as acute attention to detail which in excess leads to obsessive compulsive behaviour. Central Coherence is a type of information processing scheme that allows an individual to process information in context and pull together relevant information to develop a high-level of understanding (Hill and Frith 2003). If a person exhibits strong Central Coherence, he or she is able to take pieces of information, make connections, and extrapolate to create the "big picture" or the Gestalt. Likewise, when Central Coherence is weak, a person is unable to see the whole or the larger context, but focuses instead on the details. Individuals with ASD tend to focus on the local rather than the global. They may become entrenched in details and small components rather than the larger context. In certain instances, this type of detailed discrimination can be a strength. Some design, production, inspection, and evaluation tasks require precision and an ability to focus on details; in those instances, Weak Central Coherence is an asset. Researchers have found that individuals with ASD excel at tasks that require them to locate small features or small components within a larger picture. Individuals with ASD have the ability to focus on details, and they excel at tasks where they locate visual structures, manipulate multi-dimensional shapes, and complete visual patterns (Happé and Vital 2009; Hill and Frith 2003; Mottron 2011; Pellicano et al. 2006; Perreault et al. 2011, Samson et al. 2011). The ability to focus on specific parts helps to develop preferences and interests that can become well-rehearsed to the point of becoming obsessive in individuals with ASD. Hill and Firth (2003) indicate that the major problem with Central Coherence in ASD is the lack of study of the neuroanatomical mechanisms that could provide greater insight into behaviour and abnormal activations within the brain. Having Weak Central Coherence can be a strength; the ability to discriminate, focus intently, and attend to detail can be helpful for solving problems, analyzing systems, writing and testing software, inspecting drawings and writings for important features, and engaging in aspects of quality control.

1.2 Characteristics of Individuals with ASD

The prevalence of ASD is increasing (Autism Society of America 2014), and several comorbid conditions may exist along with a diagnosis of ASD: Depressive Disorders, Oppositional Defiance and Conduct Disorders, Anxiety Disorders, Insomnia, Seizure Disorder/Epilepsy, Sensory Integration Dysfunction, Attention Deficit Hyperactive Disorder, Attention Deficit Disorder, Tourette's Syndrome, Learning Differences, Self-Injurious Behavior, Tics, and others (Bregman 2005; Simonoff et al. 2008; Tsai 2005). The cognitive abilities of individuals with ASD vary; these individuals can be described as mentally retarded or said to have average intelligence to superior intelligence and even possess savant skills in a narrow area (Rapin and Dunn 1997). Most frequently, they are said to have splintered skills or uneven profiles of ability. Learners with autism demonstrate varying degrees of impairment in social skills, language/communication, and behavior (restrictive/repetitive/stereotypical). These three areas are often called a triad of impairment in ASD. In order to help an individual with ASD reach his or her potential, it is important to recognize the characteristics exhibited by the individual diagnosed; these include limited eye contact, phobias, anxiety, visual problems (ocular motility, saccadic eye movements, stereopsis), difficulty generalizing skills across different contexts, lack of imaginative play, splintered skills (having the ability to read, but not the ability to talk), stereotypic behaviors, and others. The next paragraphs summarize some of the most important characteristics displayed by many individuals with ASD: perseveration, sensory challenges, problems with motor skills, expressive, receptive, and pragmatic language challenges, social deficits, problems with working memory, linear execution, stereotypical behavior, a lack of academic motivation, and problems with reading comprehension.

1.2.1 Perseveration

Learners with autism tend to get lost in their thoughts and actions and appear to get stuck in an endless loop where they repeat statements, questions, or actions. They may relive an experience or ruminate until they are redirected by a new action, physical activity, or a different topic. Perseveration is frequent in ASD, and it may be the result of having rigid ideas, single-minded interests, ToM deficits, or a strong desire to communicate with limited ideas (Rapin and Dunn 1997). Dysfunction in the frontal lobe is linked with perseverative action. Sometimes negative experiences are replayed with the same fervor and emotional attachment they initially had. Tip 2: The use of computer programs and physical activities which expend energy and promote success can help an individual move past a perseverative moment.

1.2.2 Sensory Challenges and Motor Skills

Loud intense sounds or listening to a conversation with simultaneous speakers can make it difficult for a person with ASD to hear complex sounds. Hearing consonants may be difficult, and individuals who talk too fast may not be understood (Grandin and Duffy 2008). Fans, central heating and cooling systems, and noise from people in a hallway or cafeteria can be upsetting. Smells from art supplies, glue, clay or food cooking in a school cafeteria or home kitchen can cause students with ASD to become uncomfortable and even physically ill. If an individual with ASD has an aversion to glue and clay, other materials can be used to help them become expressive through art. Art activities should be enjoyable for the student rather than frustration and demanding. Drawings and sketches are not always easy for some students with ASD, so other mechanisms for creating and manipulating pictures and designs should substituted (i.e., dot-to-dot art, *ArtTouch, Xara Photo & Graphic Designer, DrawPlus, Autodesk SketchBook Pro, Google SketchUp, Corel Paint it!,* and others). Tip 3: Art activities can be used to help develop language, self-confidence, and creativity. Several easy art projects can be integrated into a students' classroom experience: the creation of collages, string designs, murals, bubble art, mobiles, and other activities (Ennis 2012). Florescent lights can flicker, upsetting the visual system and causing additional problems for some with ASD. Some students with ASD may find touch startling and uncomfortable. Normal everyday stimuli can make a day in the life of a person with ASD very challenging. Their sensory systems can be uncoordinated and produce inconsistent and unusual responses. Tip 4: Simple recorders and machines such as the Caliphone make it possible to listen to sounds, control volume, and repeat as needed. These types of devices can be used to help an individual with ASD who is disturbed by loud sounds. In addition, the devices can be used to repeat phonetic sounds, sentences, and vocabulary terms. Tip 5: Presenting uncomfortable sounds in a non-threatening environment and allowing the individual to control the intensity of the sound and the duration can help make ordinary sounds such as a vacuum cleaner, a dryer for clothing, or other household sounds more tolerable. For sounds that may be startling and unpredictable (balloons popping, fire drills, etc.), advanced notice may be necessary along with practiced routines to help the individual get used to the possibility of a startling sound.

1.2.2.1 Motor Skill Planning and Execution

Individuals with ASD may be uncoordinated or clumsy; they may drop things, have difficulty manipulating writing instruments, fall down easily because of poor balance, demonstrate poor ball handling skills, or have great difficulty with tasks that require fine and gross-motor skills (Grandin and Duffy 2008). They may find writing, drawing and tasks involving eye-hand coordination taxing. Both Kanner and Asperger described sensory-motor deficits in the individuals they observed with ASD (Whyatt and Craig 2012). Tip 6: Pencil grips, occupational therapy, tablets, and touch screens may be beneficial for students with ASD who struggle with motor activities. Apps like *Dexteria* may help individuals with ASD develop the coordination, strength, motor planning, and the execution necessary to become more proficient at motor activities. Whyatt and Craig (2012) suggest that other factors contribute to motor impairment in ASD: language ability, deficits in the use of perception (action strategies coupled with anticipatory control), and sensory-motor problems.

1.2.3 *Expressive, Receptive, and Pragmatic Language Challenges*

Most individuals with ASD have difficulty communicating their wants and needs effectively. They have varying degrees of language impairment. Without good communications skills, complete participation in social activities is impossible, and it becomes difficult to interpret invitations, respond appropriately, and engage positively with others. All of these lead to awkward interactions, isolation, and unfulfilling exchanges. It is now very popular to use tablet computers, iPads, and iPods as Augmentative and Alternative Communication Devices. Using an iPad or iPod Touch for communication costs less than traditional high-tech communications tools like the *Dynavox*. Understanding the practical aspects of language and how it is used in everyday situations can be difficult for persons with ASD. Their language challenges require experienced Speech and Language Therapists who can structure individual and group language therapy that is responsive to the needs of the individual.

In addition, language deficits present academic challenges that may impede reading comprehension and understanding. Tip 7: When presenting novel concepts, the vocabulary must be taught first and visually explained as often as possible. As an example, students with ASD studying a unit on rocks should collect rocks, examine them, and look for characteristics. Those characteristics should be used to explore and learn necessary vocabulary terms (i.e., foliated, metamorphic, sedimentary, igneous, solid, streak, mass, etc.). As much as possible, students with ASD need to experience the curriculum by visually learning and experimenting with vocabulary (i.e., making streaks with rocks, melting jelly beans to simulate what happens to metamorphic rocks, examining the porous nature of pumice rocks). Once they have the terminology, they should practice the vocabulary in the context of the educational unit (purpose, goals, discussion points, etc....), and finally, use the vocabulary and context to apply terminology. The layers of this strategy are as follows: (1) provide the student with visual and experimental opportunities to explore vocabulary; (2) present vocabulary in the context of learning new information; and (3) apply vocabulary within and outside the context in which it was learned. Graphic organizers are good tools to use to help students explore and layer knowledge. The KWL (What I **K**now, **W**ant to Learn, What I **L**earned) chart is an example that can be used; focus should be on what the student Knows and Learns as a result of the instruction.

1.2.4 Social Skills Deficits

Without social competence, people experience isolation and depression. Deficits in social reciprocity, emotional expression, and joint attention are seen in very young children with ASD; these deficits impede early learning (Scott and Baldwin 2005) and continue into adolescence and adulthood without intensive intervention. Children with ASD may not greet their parents or visually attend to them. They may not typically take an interest in their peers or make attempts to play with other children or adults. These missed opportunities lead to the development of limited social and play skills, and this impedes the child's ability to gain knowledge of more complex social interactions. There are many interventions in ASD; the well-researched interventions include Applied Behavior Analysis (ABA), Treatment and Education of Autistic and Communication Handicapped Children (TEACCH), and Picture Exchange Communication System (PECS). One controversy in ASD concerns the large number of interventions from which families can select treatment options. Some are effective, and others are not. Scott and Baldwin (2005) provide a partial list of interventions, and it contains 56 therapies that have been promoted as beneficial for young children with ASD. Having so many options is a challenge for families and doctors. Tip 8: Consult the National Autism Center for Evidence Based Interventions, and seek medical assistance from a patient, knowledgeable, and licensed health-care provider.

1.2.5 Problems with Working Memory

Working Memory allows one to manipulate information that is required for other more advanced cognitive tasks, and it involves many components (Goldstein 2011). Models have been created and used by cognitive scientists to explain and study various cognitive functions including memory. Baddeley (2000) describes a model of working memory which indicates that three components are necessary for working memory: phonological loop (holds verbal and auditory information), visuospatial sketch pad (helps in forming pictures or solving puzzles), and the central executive (determines how to divide attention between tasks required by the phonological loop, visuospatial sketch pad, and Long-Term Memory in order to accomplish a goal). Several researchers have administered clinical memory tests to children with ASD who were matched with their neurotypical counterparts. Deficits in working memory, visual memory, spatial working memory, and verbal working memory (syntax and discourse) have been found (Bennetto et al. 1996; Williams et al. 2006). Deficits in working memory in individuals with ASD can cause the person to struggle to hold in mind and manipulate relevant information (Alloway et al. 2009; Baltruschat et al. 2011). Tip 9: In order to support learners, prevent failure and working memory overload, information decomposition strategies should be used to break tasks into smaller components and simplify the nature of information that needs to be remembered. In addition, a visual representation and experience help the learner link and store relevant information.

1.2.6 Linear Execution

Learners with ASD are often said to have *tunnel vision*. One theory explaining tunnel vision proposes that the total picture is very overwhelming, and tunnel vision is a way to avoid overarousal by allowing the individual to focus on a narrow aspect of an object or situation (Boyd et al. 2007; Happé et al. 2009). Another theory is that individuals with ASD are born with a concentrated focus which can be a distraction, so they attend to one aspect of a situation. Tip 10: Learners with ASD have difficulty focusing on multiple visual cues at the same time. Structured learning situations which highlight the most important task and avoid distraction are more successful for learners with ASD. Note-taking may be difficult because of fine and gross motor skill deficits, but additionally, the acts of listening and writing or listening to multiple speakers simultaneously may present confusion and result in sensory overload for the individual with ASD. Tip 11: Instead of asking questions while a learner is engaged in an instructional video or taking notes, pause the video segment, gain the student's attention, and then ask the question. Allow learners with ASD to use a voice recorder or dictation software for notes. To promote transfer of the desired skill, provide opportunities for the student to practice the skill watched. Ask the learner questions and clarify content as needed after the presentation. Learners with ASD may find it very difficult or impossible to use more than one sensory channel simultaneously, and a single sensory channel may easily become overloaded. For example, processing and understanding speech while concentrating on an individual's facial expressions can present significant challenges. Speech-to-text software like *Dragon Dictate* may reduce the need for written activity and prevent stress and cognitive overload. A reminder system (PDA, iPad, or Smartphone) may be necessary to cue the learner into the need to review the notes, turn in homework, or gather his or her belongings. Another strategy, listening with visuals also helps clarify content.

1.2.7 Stereotypical Behavior

Routines, restrictive, and repetitive behaviors are a part of life for individuals with ASD and their families. Certain behaviors help the person with ASD react more positively to the world. Self-stimulatory behaviors (squeals and other repetitive behaviors) may seem odd or strange, and they may further isolate the individual with ASD by causing others to reject the person due to a lack of understanding.

1.2.8 Lack of Academic Motivation

Individuals with ASD many find academic work frustrating if they do not have the prerequisite skills, vocabulary, procedural or content knowledge they need. As a result, they may tune out, behave badly in an attempt to escape the demands of the task, become non-compliant or meltdown. Individuals with ASD can be taught through the use of their special interests. Preferred activities like learning capital cities of different countries, math problems, favorite movies or games, watching and operating fans, playing with gears, trains, locks, and computer games (i.e., *SimsCity, MineCraft, Star Wars, Super Mario Brothers*) on an Xbox, PS2, Nintendo DS, laptop, or tablet can be used to create instructional lessons, facilitate the development of social skills, or reinforce appropriate behavior. When engaged in a favorite activity, learners with ASD exhibit an incredible amount of focused attention. This focus can be used to educate and motivate the learner to persist through academic challenges. Tip 12: The use of a preferred item or the engagement in a preferred activity can educate, entertain, reward, or reinforce good behavior.

When it comes to education and academic tasks, children with ASD are sometimes exposed to homework and in-class assignments that are uninteresting or beyond their capability (Koegel et al. 2010). In these situations, the child may engage in disruptive behavior in an effort to avoid a boring, or challenging task. He or she may try to escape by walking or running away, engaging in perseverative language or tasks, becoming angry or aggressive, or having a meltdown. Researchers have yet to clearly identify ways to motivate children with ASD to engage in academic pursuits and persist through academic tasks they perceive as challenging or boring. In a study designed to determine whether motivational variables like natural reinforcers, choice, and maintenance tasks could be used to improve interests and academic performance, Koegel et al. (2010) found that adding motivational components to academic tasks decreased disruptive behaviors, improved interest, and resulted in faster completion rates. The researchers studied four children with ASD between the ages of 4.3–7.8 and found that academic performance improved as well as interest in learning the targeted tasks: addition, subtraction, and writing.

Tip 13: Using special interests as a teaching tool is a good strategy. If a learner with ASD loves trains, use trains to teach academic concepts like distance, time, speed, pressure, combustion, movement, and friction. A lesson on trains can incorporate videos, a virtual and/or physical field trip, and hands on activities which allow the area of special interest to be used in motivating and interesting ways. A lesson on trains can also incorporate content across academic disciplines like physics, mathematics, history, language arts, and geography. Multidisciplinary lessons anchored in real-life contexts strengthen content mastery and provide connections that produce meaningful learning. Instead of isolated and disjointed facts, components of lessons can be integrated and more easily remembered. This approach allows lessons to become memorable, useful, and easier to apply. Meaningful learning is tied to the Cognition and Technology Group at Vanderbilt (CTVG 1990), who recommended anchoring knowledge in realistic contexts and making sure knowledge was diffused and dynamically altered and used. The CTGV described most classroom knowledge as inert in that it was rarely used and rarely remembered (Roblyer and Doering 2010).

1.2.9 Problems with Reading Comprehension

The ability to read and comprehend is critical to academic success, and many individuals with ASD struggle with reading comprehension (Chiang and Lin 2007; Whalon and Hart 2011). They may have the ability to decode, and they may be fluent, but they are unable to understand, interpret, and apply what they have read. This may be due to Weak Central Coherence. Reading for meaning is complex and involves language, an understanding of social constructs, knowledge of behavior, and the ability to bring characters, settings, and relevant events into a larger context and view all of those pieces as a whole. Many students with ASD have problems with reading and other academic subjects because of deficits in language ability, social understanding, and memory. Academic achievement is variable, with students diagnosed with ASD having exceptional to very poor performance and having lower achievement levels than those predicted by their intellectual ability (Griswold et al. 2002; Estes et al. 2011). In a meta-analysis of 36 studies comparing the reading comprehension skills of individuals with ASD with those of a control group, Brown et al. (2013) indicate that may individuals struggle to comprehend highly social text and those with language deficits have the most severe reading comprehension weaknesses. The authors suggest that researchers assess language skills, semantic knowledge, decoding, and other lower-order reading skills when examining reading comprehension, as well as background knowledge necessary, processing speed, the ability to make inferences while reading, and the ability to integrate information effectively.

1.3 Technology and ASD

Technology can provide a great deal of support for individuals with ASD. In the broadest sense, technology is any electromechanical tool which can help an individual accomplish work, enjoy leisure pursuits, and get assistance. Technology can be a great aid for persons with ASD because it is customizable. It can be configured in a variety of different ways, and used to solve a variety of problems. In addition, its portability is invaluable for persons with ASD. Mobile devices make it possible for individuals with ASD to receive directions, reminders, schedules, timers, and other aids anytime and anywhere. Mobile devices provide Internet access which supplies information on a variety of topics and provides locales and directions. The devices also support social media, email, and chats, and allow an individual with ASD to continue educational pursuits and benefit from employment. Touch screens make it easy to select options and use computerized devices in a seamless way; it takes very little training to use handheld devices with a touch interface. This promotes a more intuitive interaction and reduces the learning curve. Miniaturization and lower production costs make technology tools readily available and accessible for students with ASD. Couple this with ease-of-use, flexible and engaging applications and software, multimodal presentations, predictable prompts and instructions, a rule-based structure, tactile interaction, and user control and technology tools can provide a strong and flexible environment for analyzing the needs of learners in the spectrum.

1.4 Summary

ASD is a complicated disorder that affects behavior, communication/language, and social interaction. Several theories of ASD have been discussed: Theory of Mind, Executive Dysfunction, and Weak Central Coherence to give the reader an idea of some of the dominant points of view. In addition, several characteristics of learners with ASD and technology applications have been discussed.

1.5 Discussion Points

The discussion points below are intended to help the reader review the concepts presented and reflect on the discussion in Chap. 1. Read the questions and formulate an answer.

1. Explain the theories of ASD.
2. Describe the core deficits in ASD, and explain how those impact technology use and learning.
3. Explain the "self-absorbed" nature of individuals with ASD, and relate your answer to the theories of ASD.

Chapter 2
Strategies for Supporting Students with ASD

Understanding ASD, Getting Qualified Support, and Using Technology

2.1 Introduction

Educators, parents/caregivers, and other professionals need effective strategies, procedures for positive behavior support, technologies, and evidence-based interventions that are useful for students with Autism Spectrum Disorders (ASD). Additionally, they need to understand the disability, locate qualified individuals to support and assist students, and investigate technology tools that may help students gain academic, social, and communications skills. All of these things can create more effective instruction, aid planning, impact the selection of materials, support teaching, and create a positive environment for students.

2.1.1 Understanding ASD

There are no visible signs of ASD—"He doesn't need anything—you should see some of the other kids in his class. He looks just like the other kids, don't worry."

Autism is a neurological disorder that impairs communication, social interaction, and behavior. A person in the spectrum may not have visible signs of a disability. One cannot see a neurological disorder, but it is still present (Durand 2005; Myles and Simpson 2002; Portway and Johnson 2005). The individual with ASD needs well trained personnel who have experience supporting a variety of individuals across the spectrum. Children and adults with ASD are as complex and individual as their neurotypical counterparts. The presence of ASD in an individual will manifest itself as communicative deficits, difficulty interacting with others, behavioral challenges, sensory, and social problems. The person with ASD may not appear to be visibly different from others, but assistance is still needed. Realizing that individuals with ASD have no special physical marks is just the beginning. The individual may have perfectionist tendencies, self-stimulatory behaviors, delayed echolalia, meltdowns and problems interacting with others. In addition he or she may not comply with directives they are given.

2.1.2 Perfectionist Tendencies

"But it's not perfect! It has to be perfect!"

The learner with ASD may have perfectionist tendencies. He or she may feel inadequate if his or her work is not perfect. Some children with ASD have to form the letters perfectly, work endlessly on a drawing, and erase the work again and again, if it is not 'perfect.' They will even tear their paper apart destroying their imperfect creation. They do not see the world in shades of gray like most people. Instead, things are black or white, right or wrong, yes or no. There is nothing in between. If their work is not perfectly correct, then it must be wrong, and they must try again. As they make additional attempts, they risk more frustration in their quest to 'get it right' or make it perfect.

These learners must be reminded that nothing is perfect, a good effort and a willingness to try are all that matters. Many students with ASD struggle with self-oriented perfectionism, and they display higher levels of anxiety, depression, and aggressive behavior than their neurotypical peers (Ashburner et al. 2010; Greenaway and Howlin 2010; Auger 2013). Cognitive inflexibility, impairments in reciprocal social interaction, and pragmatic language deficits may explain the dysfunctional and perfectionistic attitudes in students with ASD.

2.1.3 Self-stimulatory Behavior

Self-stimulatory behavior or stereotypy is repetitive body movement or the repetitive movement of objects that can involve one or more of an individual's senses. These behaviors (known also as *stims or self-stimulatory behaviors*) have no functional effect on the environment; they do not appear to serve a purpose, and they may be inappropriate (Foxx and Azrin 1973; Mays et al. 2011). An individual with ASD may engage in *stims* that involve their senses: smell objects, stare at objects, move fingers in his or her line of sight, lick objects, shake, rock, flap hands, pick at skin or sores, bang his or her head, repeat noises, or do other things in order to get sensory stimulation. A person with ASD can be more prone to anxiety and stress from the environment, and they may have an overly active sensory system (hypersensitivity) that is highly reactive to noises, the presence of others, sights, and smells. Their reaction to the environment coupled with their deficits processing

2.1 Introduction 17

and understanding the language and the actions of others can cause their stress level to rise, and when that happens, they engage in self-stimulatory behaviors to reduce tension or help them cope with a world they do not understand. The person may engage in self-stimulatory behaviors to calm themselves and prevent a sensory overload. An individual with a hyposensitive or underactive sensory system craves stimulation, and their self-stimulatory behaviors are thought to excite or arouse their nervous system.

A qualified occupational therapist may help individuals who are hypersensitive or hyposensitive. Walking, swinging, rolling, running, and other forms of activity may help students who need vestibular stimulation. For students who need proprioceptive stimulation pressure, squeezing, and chewing may help. The use of fidgets, brushing, and the application of deep pressure may reduce stress. Self-stimulatory behavior can interfere with learning, attending, interacting, and communicating. In addition, it can be difficult to interrupt because of the strong reinforcement it supplies (Mays et al. 2011). Boyd et al. (2012) present a topography which describes stereotypy as low and high order repetitive behaviors. Interventions for both low and high order repetitive behaviors are described and recommended practices are presented. After performing a functional behavior assessment to determine the function of the behavior, low order stereotypies can be treated using Response Blocking, Response Cost Procedures, Differential Reinforcement, Functional Communication Training, Visual Cues, and other practices. Higher order repetitive behaviors are treated using visual schedules or video-based technologies, Cognitive Behavior Therapy/Exposure Response Prevention, Differential Reinforcement of Variability, and other interventions. Additional research is needed to understand the underlying causes and mechanisms of stereotyped behaviors in ASD and useful technologies (Hodgetts et al. 2011).

2.1.4 Delayed Echolalia

After sliding a bottle of Sweet Leaf Tea across the checkout counter in a local grocery store, a young man with ASD told the cashier "whiskey please!"

Echolalia is an automatic and unintentional behavior that is apparent in ASD. It is the repetition of someone else's words and phrases in either an attempt to make social contact when language is beyond the individual's level of competence, or parroting that does not fit the social context (Prizant and Rydell 1984). It is an imitative behavior that can occur immediately after the initial presentation of an utterance or a significant time after the utterance (Grossi et al. 2013). When the phrase is repeated a significant time after the utterance, it is called delayed echolalia. Echolalia is present in ASD and other neurological and psychiatric conditions. When echolalia is delayed, a student with ASD will know that they should respond, but find themselves at a loss for words. Sometimes the student may want to request an object or lodge a protest, but the words do not come. These are times when a student will repeat language they have heard and memorized from a cartoon, a western, or a TV commercial. Phrases from westerns like "You're a bad, bad, man!" "Hold it right there mister!" "Whiskey!" "No one can stop me, HA HA!" are examples of delayed echolalia or scripts used by a 10 year-old with ASD who has a fascination with westerns. Some researchers consider echolalia to be a part of normal language development, but others feel that it is a behavior that might interrupt the normal linguistic and cognitive development of a learner. Prizant and Rydell (1984) indicated that delayed echolalia served several functions that were interactive or non-interactive, appeared with or without comprehension, and contained varying degrees of relevance to situations and linguistic contexts. The categories of non-interactive delayed echolalia: non-focused (self-stimulatory), situation associations, rehearsal, self-directive, and non-interactive labeling. Interactive delayed echolalia fell into the following categories: turn-taking, verbal completion, labeling, imparting information, calling, affirming, requests, protests, and directives.

Hetzroni and Tannous (2004) created a computer-based simulation which allowed students to interact in three settings: play, food, and hygiene. Practice in the simulated settings had a positive impact on all students' functional communication. Improvements in functional communication were documented, irrelevant speech, delayed, and immediate echolalia decreased, and more appropriate speech was observed in each of the intervention settings. Four of the five participants had a noticeable change in communicative initiations, and each participant preferred the interactive computer simulation. In addition, the researchers noticed generalization of correct functional language to the classroom setting.

2.1.5 Meltdowns and Their Meaning

"But I don't want to do division! I want to do multiplication! I hate division!"

The behavior of individuals with ASD can be challenging and explosive at times. Depending on the person, angry and aggressive outbursts can include kicking, hitting, and even fighting. Sometimes meltdowns can be averted, if the person's triggers are known. The only way to discover the triggers is to observe the person, and take careful records of behavior prior to, during, and after the incident. If the individual is verbal and able to articulate his or her feelings, he or she may be able to explain why the angry outburst occurred. Parents or caregivers should be consulted to share their experiences, formulate a plan of action, and provide assistance. Since ASD is a spectrum of disorders, varying degrees of language impairment are present. Some individuals are non-verbal, and some struggle with pragmatic, expressive, and/or receptive language. The inability to communicate effectively can cause extreme frustration and anxiety that can cause a meltdown. Sometimes physical or psychological factors trigger a meltdown. Some of the more common signs of distress that may precede a meltdown are as follows: rubbing the eyes, using loud repetitive language, demonstrating confusion, tearing, picking the skin

2.1 Introduction 19

on the body, crying, hitting, kicking, or disengaging in tasks. When the signs of a meltdown are present, it is necessary to simplify the task, reduce the demand, and help the individual complete the task. Allowing the individual to escape the task allows the person to make an incorrect association. If tactics to escape a non-preferred task are successful, the learner will repeat those actions each time he or she is confronted with a non-preferred task. Children in the spectrum are very observant, and they often recognize patterns and make associations which become their expectation. If these expectations are not confirmed, it makes them upset and fearful and they may have a meltdown.

Meltdowns can be caused by incorrect associations, hunger, fear, isolation, the memory an unpleasant event, over-stimulation, frustration, exhaustion, chemical imbalance, mistreatment, the inability to communicate, stress, unpredictable events and other things. Some meltdowns can be triggered by demands that push the individual beyond his or her level of competence and capability. In the introductory phrase, the child with Autism was having a meltdown because he had mastered multiplication facts, and he expected to continue with multiplication rather than learn something new—division. He was not comfortable with division or learning any other math skill. He preferred multiplication exercises because they were familiar, safe, predictable, and easy. Each time a math activity was presented that contained division, a meltdown ensued. Once the student understood that math time could be associated with other types of problems, and he realized that multiplication was the inverse of division, his comfort level increased, and he did a better job.

Novel situations and activities, crowded shelves, colorful material, opened doors and shelves, and noise can induce stress in individuals with ASD and trigger anxiety which may lead to a meltdown (Lytle and Todd 2009). Familiarity, multiple presentations of information and instructions, checks for student understanding, planned activities, routines, choice, and realistic expectations can reduce stress and anxiety. Instruction in social skills and language can also reduce problem behaviors (Macintosh and Dissanayake 2006; Mancil et al. 2009; Scattone et al. 2002).

If the meltdown cannot be diverted, it is better to calmly work through it with the student. Tip 14: Remain patient and keep a low to moderate tone of voice. Realize that the child is having a difficult time, and he or she is not trying to hurt or threaten anyone. Poor reactions on the part of all involved parties can extend and escalate rather than diffuse this difficult situation. Try to redirect the student to activities that take his or her mind off the meltdown, and prepare for it to 'run its course.' Meltdowns are not teachable moments; they are just times to endure with patience and resolve. It is ill advisable to try to teach content, reason with the student, or try punitive measures.

2.1.6 Facilitating Positive Social Interaction

A note from one classmate to another—both have ASD: "Dear Friend, The teacher just stole my samurai helmet. That is a crime. So we should have a rebellion against the school and the teachers. Do you want to join? Circle Yes No From S."

This note between two friends is cute. Teachers should make it a point to recognize the social needs of the student with ASD and try to help them work with their peers. It is good to share both disappointments and triumphs with others. Social relationships are important; they help reduce stress and isolation, and they add meaningful interaction and a sense of connectedness. Social skills need to be explicitly taught to individuals in the Autism Spectrum. With the support of other students with ASD and neurotypical peers, students with ASD can learn to make eye contact, use appropriate gestures, behave well, and develop age-appropriate language. Rotating buddies can help alleviate stress, increase language skills, and support the student with Autism. Tip 15: Involve the child's peers in positive and consistent support. They can be a resource for the child and help the child manage in the classroom. Having the child's neurotypical peers compliment him and providing opportunities for peer mentoring, tutoring, and assistance may help the child with ASD feel like a valued member of the class, and these practices may lessen problem behavior. Applied Behavior Analysis (ABA) approaches for teaching social skills have been demonstrated to be very effective at teaching initiations and discrete social responses (Weiss 2013).

Mancil et al. (2009) examined the effects of a social story (intervention for improving social interaction by Carol Gray) presented in PowerPoint™ on the aberrant behaviors of three children with ASD during recess and transitions. They also examined the difference between social stories presented on paper versus those presented with PowerPoint™. The aberrant behaviors decreased, and the PowerPoint version of the social story (*CASST*) produced slightly better results than the paper version. The researchers suggest that the use of the computer's visual prompts to read and listen to the story and visuals may have provided additional support that helped maintain student attention. Additional research was suggested, because of the small sample size, but positive features of the intervention were as follows: easy implementation by teachers, preparation was not time-intensive, independent use by students, and the ability to embed the activities into the students' daily routines. Other forms of technology have also been used to teach social understanding, rules, and judgment. Results are promising for the use of virtual reality, interactive intelligent agents, and video modeling (Mitchell et al. 2007; Barakova et al. 2009).

2.1.7 Securing Compliance

"Will you do this for me? No… I don't know how."

Individuals in the spectrum need to understand the expectations of others as well as acceptable rules and procedures. They need prerequisite skills, realistic expectations, and assistance that secures their cooperation. It is important that rapport is established before making demands on a student with ASD. It is necessary to

2.1 Introduction

understand the person, their reinforcers, needs, preferences, and interaction patterns before demanding that they perform a specific task. Many individuals in the spectrum are very sensitive, and they may be trying to overcome negative experiences. They may need to work through negative feelings and associations before they can establish trust and participate cooperatively. Tip 16: Clearly explaining the task or activity and describing the steps involved, checking for understanding by asking questions and observing responses, and providing sufficient time for interpreting, processing and executing the request are helpful.

Cooperation on the part of the individual with ASD is very important. Personalized instruction based on high-interest areas, family involvement in educational planning, and the use of the high-preference strategy (presenting two to three preferred academic tasks before presenting a non-preferred academic task) may ensure student compliance (Banda and Kubina 2010).

2.2 Getting Qualified Support

"You will have a classroom aide assigned next year. She is very good; we are lucky to have her. You should probably contact her over the summer break. She will probably work with you before school starts. In fact, I will touch bases with her, and then send you her number."

Experience and training are good prerequisites for working with a person diagnosed with ASD. Untrained paraprofessionals can impede social skill development and acceptance, create confusion, and promote overdependence (Zager and Shamow 2005). The experienced professional or paraprofessional should spend time with the child or adult and his/her family and learn as much as possible. Understanding the current reinforcers, non-preferred activities, language and level of academic skills is critical. The individual providing support should know how to collect performance data and modify the environment to ensure success. Paraprofessionals in this role must be well trained; they should be an advocate for the child, a coach when necessary, a mentor, and a helper. They should work with families and members of the school staff to facilitate the development of language skills and social relationships. At stressful points in the individual's school day (recess, lunch, transitions to and from special activities like music, art, and school sponsored events), the child's aide should provide a safety net of assistance, encouragement, and reassurance. The individual providing support should build confidence, promote independence, provide structure and routine, assist with difficult tasks, and reduce the anxiety and sensory overload of the individual with ASD. Strong systems of support neutralize the isolation, anxiety, and depression of those with ASD (Brewin and Renwick 2008; Marshall 2002; Muskat 2005, Rayner 2005).

2.2.1 Voting People off the Island

"School should be like Total Drama Island, where I can vote people off. My teacher said it would be sad if people got voted off the island."

Teachers and others working with individuals in the spectrum should be aware of sensory issues, use direct language, use positive reinforcement, and gain the attention of the learner. Additionally, they should be aware of the theories of ASD, and the characteristics of the learner. Each of these was discussed in Chap. 1. Teachers want all students to be successful. Teachers want them to enjoy learning and appreciate the opportunity. Teachers do not want to leave anyone behind or vote anyone off the educational island, because knowledge is power and it liberates, promotes self-sufficiency and freedom. Knowledge makes the difference in life by providing the ability to change one's status in life and make choices that are beneficial.

2.2.2 Sensory Issues

Learning situations can be difficult for students with ASD, because many have sensory integration dysfunction. The hypersensitive student may avoid touch and hear lights humming, coughing, other children talking, the A/C, the pencil sharpener, and the teacher talking simultaneously and have difficulty filtering these sounds. The smell of glue, play dough, markers, and lunch being prepared in the cafeteria might be enough to make the person with ASD uncomfortable, ill, or even unresponsive to instruction. The hyposensitive student may seek out stimulation by touching objects or spinning. Teachers must not ignore the sensory issues that hinder students with ASD from participating and behaving appropriately.

2.2.2.1 Case Example 1

In one classroom, a child in the spectrum cringed and refused to write information displayed by an overhead projector. The child's aide said "he can see that, his eyes are not as old as mine." How can the aide know what that child can see? She cannot view the world through his eyes. She thought he was being obstinate. As it turned out, the child had visual issues that made it difficult for him to view and write projected information. Teachers must make an effort to be sensitive to this issue and consult with other professionals to find ways to make the student more comfortable.

2.2.3 Using Direct Language

The KISS Principle reminds people to keep things simple. In addition to an awareness of sensory issues, individuals working with students diagnosed with ASD must communicate with the student in simple and direct terms. Slang, sarcasm, idioms, colloquialisms, and jokes are not well understood by individuals in the spectrum. It is better to use clear, direct language. Tip 17: Don't say, "Turn your completed assignment in." Instead say, "Put your papers in the orange box on my desk." Don't say, "Let's call it a day." Instead say, "We are finished." Short, simple statements are better than detailed instructions. After giving an instruction in clear language, give the student time to respond. Many students with ASD have auditory processing delays, and it may take them more time to comply with requests.

2.2.4 Using Positive Reinforcement

Individuals with ASD need to be rewarded for their efforts to behave appropriately, integrate, engage, and overcome their many challenges. Praise, checkmarks, stickers, and opportunities to engage in preferred activities are all examples of positive reinforcement. Pleasant and affirming rewards reinforce desired behavior and motivate students to repeat the desired behaviors. Tip 18: Reinforcers should not be overused; they should be changed as the student changes so that they will remain effective.

2.2.5 Gaining the Learner's Attention

It is necessary to get the student's attention before asking him/her to complete a task. Facing the student and telling him/her what is needed using simple and direct language is an effective practice. Following that with a check for understanding to make sure the student understands what is expected is helpful (Zager and Shamow 2005). It is critical to gain the student's attention, and give the student time to process requests. Tip 19: Time the student with ASD to see how long it takes for him or her to execute a directive. Many times, the students will not have difficulty executing, but they may need extra time to process the request. Language and the ability to understand it are critical keys for successful execution, and students with ASD have problems understanding language.

2.2.6 Understanding the Theories that Attempt to Explain ASD

"He just won't leave her alone, and she told him to stop!"

An angry guidance counselor aware that the male student had ASD did not understand ToM in the quote above.

2.2.6.1 Case Example 2

A 3rd grade male with ASD kept bothering his classmate. 'Bothering' was the term the guidance counselor used, because the male student kept trying to get his classmate's attention during class, even after being told to stop. The counselor did not understand that the male student was not purposefully trying to agitate or harm his classmate. He had no idea that his classmate had different desires, opinions, feelings, and interests from his own. He wanted to engage with his classmate by playing a game they played often; he simply did not understand that his classmate wanted to participate in the class activity by following the teacher's directions. Individuals with ASD have deficits in their ability to understand the intentions of others. They have difficulty reciprocating socially and understanding the effects of their behavior on others. Simon Baron-Cohen proposed and documented deficits in ToM in children with Autism. He first used the term mind-blindness to explain why social interaction is challenging for individuals with ASD. Basically, individuals in the spectrum may not gather enough information (from social and environmental queues, emotions, gestures, facial features) to help them develop an awareness of what another person might think, feel, need or want. In addition, many individuals with ASD also have difficulty understanding their own feelings, motives, thoughts, and needs. The young man in Case Example 2 could not put himself in his classmate's shoes or view the world from her eyes. His own lenses were the only vantage point he could use to assess the situation.

2.2.7 *Learning to Handle Non-preferred Activities*

All persons have non-preferred activities, and students in the spectrum are no different. A student in the spectrum may be cognitively inflexible, and it may be more difficulty for him or her to attempt non-preferred activities. This situation takes a great deal of patience, positive reinforcement, and encouragement. The student's refusal may have roots in insecurity, fear, or a lack of knowledge. It is important to address these areas first. If the student is not psychologically safe, he or she will be unwilling to try a non-preferred activity. Tip 20: Do not automatically lower expectations for students with ASD; assume average intelligence, unless documentation is present indicating otherwise. Provide support and 'think outside the box.' Using manipulatives, breaking processes into smaller steps, and demonstrating requirements are beneficial practices. Having students work on small steps and gradually increasing the complexity is necessary along with extrinsic rewards and encouragement during the learning process. Using things that reinforce the child in order to secure compliance and determining whether or not the student's refusal is due to a sensory issue are important.

2.2.7.1 Case Example 3

During a classroom visit, a 2nd grader was observed who refused to do art activities - art was definitely a non-preferred activity. After talking with the teacher and visiting the classroom several times, it was apparent that the smells, sounds, and textures of the medium were problematic. When the children did drawings, perfectionist tendencies surfaced in this student. His drawings were not like those he saw his peers create and submit. His behavior became negative, and he became angry and unwilling to do any of the activities in art. After talking with the art teacher, other activities were created and substituted to help the child become successful in the art class: dot-to-dot drawings, numeric picture puzzles, step-by-step drawings, stencil creations, models, and activities using tracing paper. A little creativity and patience changed the art experience from a negative to a positive for this student. After a six-week period, the student's unsatisfactory marks and behavior in art became satisfactory, and art became more tolerable.

2.3 Applications of Technology

Technology is sometimes called a great equalizer—that can be true for individuals with the ability to afford and access tools that meet their needs. Computerized tools can liberate users from drudgery, connect users with expertise, permit access to vast amounts of data, and facilitate online learning. Many learners individuals with ASD gravitate toward technology (Barakova et al. 2009; Mancil et al. 2009). The visual appeal and locus of control are some of the factors that make technology appealing for individuals with ASD. There are many applications of technology in Autism Research: systems for data collection, video for monitoring behavior and developing social skills, electronic data transmission to professionals, apps on tablets, smartphones, and other personal devices, Computer-Assisted Training (Instruction), virtual reality, intelligent agents, and more. Goodwin (2008) discusses a variety of technology applications that can assist individuals with Autism, practitioners, and researchers. Personal records of behavior can be video-taped, and the observations can be sent to a behavior analyst to help determine triggers and situations that cause inappropriate or difficult behavior in an individual with ASD. Computerized tools such as apps, video, and PDAs may help individuals with ASD learn to recognize emotions, generalize skills, communicate, grasp academic content, and organize information.

The IAN Community, an online research and implementation site (https://www.ianresearch.org/) is another example of the use of technology that fosters worldwide collaboration and research for persons with ASD and their families. IAN supports researchers by linking their research questions and instruments with families willing to provide data and answer queries. IAN maintains a comprehensive online library of the latest research, and serves as a place for meeting, sharing, and examining issues and solutions. Another application of technology in ASD is speech-to-text programs. These tools allow users with ASD to transform speech into text; speech recognition software can be valuable for note taking, preparing reports and written compositions. Synthesis and voice transformation research creates diagnostic, remedial, and assistive methods for the production of speech by individuals with ASD who are non-verbal or have limited language ability.

The development, dissemination, and use of technology is encouraged by Autism Speaks' Innovative Technology for Autism (ITA) initiative. ITA is at the forefront of development, advocacy, mentoring, treatment, and knowledge of ASD. The organization also supports technology use by researchers, developers, teachers, clinicians, and families in an effort to improve the educational, social, communicative, and functional outcomes for individuals in the autism spectrum. The url for the ITA is http://www.autismspeaks.org/science/research/initiatives/ita_initiative.php.

The popularity, affordability, and portability of technology has increased interest in its use as an intervention tool in Autism. The earliest use of computers with individuals with ASD occurred in the 1970s, and even then, positive results were reported. Since that time, technology has become more widespread and more affordable, so the use of Computer-Assisted Training or Computer-Assisted Instruction (CAT/CAI) and other forms of technology for intervention planning in ASD has increased. In the 1970s only one or two studies were published in peer-reviewed journals, but by 2010 that number had grown to about 40 (Ploog et al. 2013). Parental blogs reporting anecdotal benefits from computers used to teach individuals with ASD also added to the interest in formally assessing technology tools to determine their value for individuals with ASD (Ploog et al. 2013). Two critical questions are often asked in research on technology interventions in ASD—most studies are investigating whether or not the technology intervention is effective, and some studies are comparing technology interventions to traditional teaching and training methods.

Many of the studies have positive reports that are promising, but technology in ASD is considered a new frontier and a young science that requires cautious interpretation and rigorous ongoing research. Most studies utilize small sample sizes, do not present operational definitions of the independent and dependent variables, and only take a first step in the form of an exploratory or descriptive analysis to set the stage for more rigorous investigations. As a result, many researchers are not yet ready to consider CAT an evidence-based intervention for individuals with ASD (Bölte et al. 2010; Clark and Choi 2005; Pennington 2010; Wainer and Ingersoll 2011). Follow-up studies are needed with control conditions, comparisons of the effects of different treatment approaches, matching participants across conditions, and comparisons with traditional training methods (Ploog et al. 2013).

Some additional applications of technology include the following: listening centers, video modeling, reading software, e-books, the creation of comic strip conversations, electronic tools for reading, writing, typing, mathematics instruction, and vocabulary acquisition, talking calculators, talking photo albums (steps in a process, recognition of facts, places, people, emotions), software for emotional recognition, instructional software for academic enrichment, distance learning courses, augmentative communication devices, card readers and recorders, personal digital assistants (PDAs), mobile phones, customizable overlays for computerized input, Nintendo DS (math and reading games), virtual reality (Reaction Grid and Second Life for older learners), tablet applications, AAC, and others. When technology tools are well aligned with desired learning outcomes, they can effectively support teaching and learning in engaging and interesting ways. Different forms of technology can support learners in the spectrum, and make it possible for them to learn in more visually appealing and more entertaining formats.

2.4 Summary

It is a mistake to judge a student with ASD based on his or her appearance. Thorough evaluations by groups of professionals should be undertaken along with careful observations across multiple settings. In addition, parental information can provide additional information to help explain the student with ASD. It is important to understand the student's challenges and preferences in order to select instructional materials and computerized tools and provide appropriate support which targets the student's individual needs. Individuals with ASD need varying degrees of communicative, social, academic, and behavioral support in order to succeed. They may have perfectionist tendencies, demonstrate self-stimulatory behaviors, have problems complying with directives, demonstrate challenges understanding others, and have problems dealing with non-preferred activities. Computerized tools can be used to provide academic, language, and social skills support.

2.5 Discussion Points

These discussion questions are a form of self-check, review, and reflection. Answer the questions to examine your knowledge and your perception of learners with ASD. Review the Case Examples and determine the course of action you would have taken.

1. Explain why individuals with ASD may demonstrate challenging behavior.
2. Are there strengths that individuals with ASD demonstrate?
3. What learning strategies might be effective for learners with ASD?

Chapter 3
Family Issues in ASD

Problems Areas and Technology Use

3.1 Introduction

In Chap. 1 the theories behind ASD were discussed and some of the characteristics of learners with ASD were described. Chapter 2 presented practical considerations for working with individuals with ASD; those considerations must be applied in the home. Sensory Integration Dysfunction, problems with motor skills, expressive, receptive and pragmatic language deficits, lack of social skills, limited cognitive flexibility, executive dysfunction, and problem behavior must be monitored and worked with at home. Practical wisdom and explanations from mothers of children with ASD are included in this chapter to further illuminate the challenges: stress, educating the child with ASD, preparing for the future, dealing with sibling issues, managing parental involvement in education and therapy programs, behavior of the child with ASD, and the use of technology.

3.1.1 Increased Stress

Here are a few typical expressions of the stress involving with having a child with ASD:

> It's a 24/7 job regardless of where I may be. The financial and marital stress from having a child with ASD is more than any other type of stress I've experienced. There is no such thing as a 'good night's sleep,' we may never be 'empty nesters,' and the worry about what will happen to her when we are no longer able to care for her is constant.

> Stress is never ending. Just when you move through one problem or crisis, another one pops up. We need people to help with everyday care issues. One size fits all programs do not work. We need help early on when they are young so that maybe they won't need it later.

> How stressful it is not having personal and/or school/state resources for assistance; how psychologically oppressive it is to feel that our child's future depends solely on our research, our interventions, and our decisions—there is really no one professional to turn to for information and guidance.

Families caring for children with ASD experience a great deal of stress; their stress level is higher than that of families caring for children with other disabilities (Gray 2006; Myers et al. 2009; Silva and Schalock 2012). Many factors contribute to the stress a family experiences: severity of the child's impairment, comorbid medical conditions, personal finances, work issues, challenges understanding the child, caring for the needs of the child, and the inability to balance all of the demands. Multiple factors interact simultaneously to cause parents additional anxiety and stress.

The severity of the child's impairment causes stress. Parents whose children are more severely impaired report more stress and tension than parents whose children are less severely impaired by ASD (Tobing and Glenwick 2007). Mothers of children with ASD have been found to have poorer mental and physical health and a lower quality of life than mothers of typically developing children (Myers et al. 2009; Ingersoll and Hambrick 2011; Schwichtenberg and Poehlmann 2007). Comorbid conditions contribute to maternal stress. Individuals with ASD may have abnormal sensory responses, gastrointestinal disorders, self-injurious behavior, aggression and irritability, sleep disturbances, coordination and motor planning difficulties, attention regulation problems, an insistence on sameness, heightened anxiety, detailed focus, seizures, problems with learning and cognition, and other problems that compound stress (Silva and Schalock 2012; Cox et al. 2012). All of these problems require attention, and many require specialized support from a Behavior Analyst, a Psychiatrist, a Developmental Pediatrician, a Neurologist, Psychologist, and other well-trained professionals. These additional evaluations and services increase the cost of caring for a child with ASD and raise the stress level of a family. The cost of educating a child with ASD is a challenge for public schools; the cost in the USA may be $20,000 USD per year with the most intensive interventions costing as much as $100,000 USD or more per student per year (Gray and Brann 2014). Parents who choose other non-public educational options in the USA may select private therapeutic schools, charter schools, or home schools.

After being stressed at home, most parents go to work and encounter demands in the workplace. Deadlines, extra assignments, and challenges at work add another level of stress to the parent of a child with ASD. After meeting the demands of the workplace, the parent goes home to the demands there. All of these factors explain the higher stress level of parents of individuals with ASD. Understanding the person with ASD, caring for the needs of that individual, and supporting a marriage, friendships, and other familial relationships can be difficult to balance.

Since ASD persists throughout an individual's lifetime, the stress is typically ongoing from childhood through adulthood (Myers et al. 2009). As the child moves through developmental phases, there are increasing concerns for the child's safety, psychological, mental, and physical well-being, coping mechanisms, level of support, and the development of life skills and possibly employment skills. Parents who made the statements quoted above were asked what they wished others knew about their life with a child with ASD. They indicated that their stress level was constant. They had limited resources; their marriages were under additional pressure; they lacked sleep; their child might be with them until their demise; and there were always new challenges. They indicated that early intervention was critical in their child's early years, and receiving that intervention could make the difference in their child's long-term progress and success. Additionally, they highlighted the need for competent and comprehensive professional assistance to help them sort through the issues and provide support for the myriad of challenges. These concerns are mirrored in the literature (Brewin et al. 2008; Fleischmann 2004; Hoffman et al. 2008). Other comments from parents are provided below; these further explain the reasons for the increased stress parents feel.

"I cannot even begin to describe my life to other people. I wish others knew how hard it is to receive no extra help. My insurance company specifically excludes any treatment, even augmentative communications devices for autism. The school staff is in complete denial of the need to train the teachers and therapists who work with our kids. We get no extra assistance, because our income is too high. The waiting list for benefits like CLASS is approximately 7 years. It is very frustrating." CLASS stands for Community Living Assistance and Support Services. It is available in Texas under the Department of Aging and Disability Services.

> It's harder than it looks, that even if he looks normal at first glance, there are so many aspects to it once you get to know him. It's very draining financially and that has an effect on my marriage, and not always a good one either.

> I wish they knew how much I love my child with ASD, but how hard it is to try to provide him with what he needs when the resources are not there. I wish they knew how hard it is to meet the needs of every member of my family at the same time and yet be the only one responsible for my son's dreams and future. I wish they knew how scary the thought of dying is for a parent of a child with ASD.

3.1.2 Educational Challenges

The vast majority of children with ASD are educated in public school settings in the USA. American public school systems are usually the first place parents go to find educational support and diagnostic testing for their children with ASD. Stoner et al. (2005) indicate that the relationship between parents of children with ASD and educational professionals is a critical issue in Special Education due to litigation involving parents and the legal mandates of The Individuals with Disabilities Education Act that requires parental involvement in the education of their children with disabilities. Interaction between parents and educators has been poorly integrated and riddled with tension, confusion and frustration (Lake and Billingsley 2000). This situation exists because parents have been viewed by educational professionals as obstacles to their child's education, adversaries, or marginal entities that are expected to provide little input (Ivey 2004; Turnbull and Turnbull 2001). Parents, on the other hand, have viewed educational professionals as difficult and uncollaborative (Dunlap et al. 1994). Stoner et al. (2005) reported that all parents in their study responded negatively or conditionally when they were asked whether or not they trusted the educational professionals with whom they interacted. This lack of trust was related to experiences the parents had with educators.

Educational testing takes about 90 days in most schools, and students with ASD have to be tested and qualify for placement in Special Education Programs. Students do not receive accommodations until the testing documenting their disabilities and needs is performed. Ninety days can be a long time for a child with ASD who is struggling in a classroom setting that may present sensory challenges, have a large student to teacher ratio, and have a teacher who many not have knowledge of ASD or experience working with students in the spectrum. A free and appropriate public education in the least restrictive setting can be very overwhelming for an individual with ASD without well-trained individuals who provide support at a variety of levels: social skills development and differentiated instruction.

Quality of life at school is another issue of concern for parents of children with ASD. Are children with ASD involved in positive ways with their peers? Are the children with ASD participants in the instructional process? Are children with ASD socially accepted and included by their peers, and are they learning skills that prepare them for life? These are typical questions any parent would ask of school personnel. To find answers, the role of the staff, teachers, and other school professionals must be examined. In addition, the nature of interactions with the child, the structure and services provided need to be examined.

Parents feel that staff, teachers, and other school professionals play an important role in the education of their child; these professionals are gatekeepers for accessing services that are needed, and they are helpful when they respect the child and provide individualized services and use effective practices (Brewin et al. 2008). Tip 21: Examples of effective practices include the following: preparing the student for transitions or changes in the schedule, using predictable daily routines or schedules prepared in visual or written form, providing breaks, and permitting physical activity throughout the day to lessen anxiety and improve the child's ability to cope with sensory issues that may be aggravated by the environment. Stoner et al. (2005) indicated that parents reported that staff, teachers, and other school professionals lacked consistent training and awareness of ASD. Many did not recognize sensory issues or understand how ASD affected students. Most school personnel had little or no training on ASD, and they lacked a collaborative attitude with parents. The parents further indicated that school personnel made obtaining services difficult and confusing, and they did not provide enough specialized services or links to services offered outside the school environment (Brewin et al. 2008; Stoner et al. 2005).

Positive social interactions with peers can make the school experience positive and meaningful for students with ASD. Often, their language difficulties, inability to understand and predict the behaviors of others (due to a ToM deficit), cognitive inflexibility, and literal interpretations cause them to experience bullying and social isolation. Sometimes their motor skill deficits and executive function challenges make it difficult for them to physically keep pace with other students. Add to that their self-stimulatory behavior, and narrow interests, and students with ASD are not seen as the 'cool kids' or social butterflies that other students seek out. Other children may not be able to relate to them, because of their narrow interests and their inability to focus on topics outside of their area of special interest. Persons with ASD may perseverate on items or topics, and this widens the social acceptance gap. Social skills training and integration with peers is needed, and teachers may not have the training to facilitate this type of special training. Teachers and other school personnel may also need training which helps them relate to the student with ASD and learn how to use the student's interests to integrate him or her into educational pursuits and social groups.

The structure of the educational environment should be flexible, adaptable to the child, and filled with varying approaches and supports. One structural component, the aid, special needs assistant, or paraprofessional is very helpful for students who need more one-on-one assistance and support. Tip 22: The instructional aid or paraprofessional must be well-trained and he or she must understand the individual student's needs, strengths, and weaknesses. This person must be able to provide a varying amount of support on a daily basis to help the student with ASD achieve success in the school environment. Without appropriate and consistent support, depression, loneliness, and isolation are felt by the young adults and children with ASD (Brewin et al. 2008; Portway and Johnson 2005). These negative experiences can increase negative behaviors and cause the student to have negative feelings about school which impede learning and further progress. It would be helpful if the school environment was linked with other services and other agencies that provide support. This would be helpful for students transitioning out of secondary programs into community involvement and employment (Brewin et al. 2008).

Parents of individuals with ASD are under a great deal of stress, and school personnel do not always recognize the parent's difficult position. Parents want the best for their children and they are willing to work cooperatively with others who have their child's best interest in mind. Educators and parents should listen to each other, respect each other, and work collaboratively to create programs and support that will benefit the student with ASD. If more cooperation were present, the opportunities would be better for children with ASD. The comments below indicate the struggles some parents faced obtaining a free and appropriate education. From the parents' perspectives, obtaining services is a fight, using the 'right' teaching techniques is essential, more resources are needed in schools, and advocacy is critically needed to help learners with ASD.

> How difficult it is to fight the school system to get an appropriate and safe education setting for your child. How much potential children on the spectrum have, it just takes the right techniques to reach autistics. How unfair it is that insurance and the schools won't help.

I have to argue with the school system to get the basic services my child needs and deserves.

Children with autism can learn to relate to others. More resources offered through schools would improve the lives of children with autism and probably other students also. There are multiple stressors for families when the child has autism; there is also a lot of joy seeing them improve and learn. Autistic kids are extremely hard workers who want to do their best.

How hard it is to constantly advocate to the school system on the importance of their well-being. How easy [it is] to turn the other cheek when dealing with the aggression etc.... It's not something you can take away with a pill. There needs to be advocacy [and] more people looking out for these kids especially during adolescence.

3.1.3 The Future

Ask any parent of a child with ASD about the future, and you will hear responses that indicate that parents of individuals with ASD have more concern, fear, and apprehension about the future than parents of typically developing children. Here are representative comments indicating that fact:

> It is a life-long disability. My child will never live independently; we need to have highly trained individuals care for our child in our absence and it is often times difficult to find people. Many parents are unable to afford the services needed to improve the quality of life of their child and family.

> We worry about his future and wonder if he will ever be able to live on his own, hold down a job, and have a lasting relationship, if that is what he chooses for himself.

> If there will be something for him to do under supervision when he is out of public school—will he be okay and cared for when we die?

> I wish I could say that I am a better person because I have a son with ASD, but I don't feel that way. I worry so much about his future and what will happen to him when I die. I worry if I will save enough to have in a trust for him and wonder if I have given him the best.

Most parents look forward to the self-sufficiency of their children. Parents typically prepare their children to enter the world as a contributing citizen who nurtures his or her own family and provides opportunities for individuals in his or her community. It is an ongoing circle of life, and it is predictable and expected for most adults, but this cycle is interrupted and drastically altered when parents have a child or children with ASD. The normal process of 'leaving and cleaving' does not occur. The parent of a child with ASD must face the reality that their child may never live independently. The child will grow into an adult who needs a varying amount of constant and consistent support in order to function. This is the cruel reality for parents of children with ASD. Parents worry about their child's future—who will care for their adult child with ASD? How will he or she live, what will be his or her quality of life; what happens when the parents die? These difficult questions are with parents as they struggle to help their children learn and grow into adulthood. Many parents create disability trusts and assign guardians in order to help relieve some of this stress. They save the money they can, get on waiting lists for services, and seek out programs that may help their child gain skills that an employer may need. Some parents also establish businesses from which their child can benefit, and most undertake grueling therapy schedules in order to work on a variety of problems: social, self-regulatory, and communications skills.

3.1.4 Sibling Issues

According to Rivers and Stoneman (2003), studies on the effects of children having a sibling with ASD are mixed. Both positive and negative findings have been reported. Some of the negative reports have included loneliness, problems with the sibling's behavior, less reciprocal social interaction with the sibling, and internalizing and externalizing their sibling's problems (Bägenholm and Gillberg 1991; Fisman et al. 2000; Knott et al. 1995). Some of the positive results were acceptance on the part of siblings, more warmth expressed by those with a sibling with ASD, the ability to act as a social agent for their sibling with ASD, and admiration for the sibling with ASD, (Roeyers and Mycke 1995; Kaminsky and Dewey 2001). Many parents are aware of the long-term needs of their child with ASD, and they do not want the child's typically developing sibling to have to care for the child with ASD. Here are some typical statements involving siblings:

"I don't want S. to have to take care of A. That's why I work so hard getting A. therapy. I want S to have a life." (S is the sister of A, and A has Asperger Syndrome.)

> Not only do you have to balance yourself for your kids, but you have to balance the world for your kids.

Parents are keenly aware of the needs of the child with ASD, and they are also aware that more of their resources and attention go to the child with ASD rather than their neurotypical child or children. The following comment illustrates this point. "… I put more energy and effort and time and tears into raising my one child with Asperger's than most people could handle—… he is more work than my 3 little neurotypical children combined."

3.1.5 Parental Involvement in Educational and Therapy Programs

Here is what some parents say about their involvement:

> Being a parent is a hard job, having a child with Autism is very hard, but so rewarding when the breakthroughs come. I feel lucky to have my child; he has opened doors for me where I can look at things a little differently than I might have otherwise.

> Work hard every day. It is so worth it! My child is 12; he grows and learns every day. Our quality of life is SO much better now, than when our son was 3. You must do the work to reap the benefits. The disability will not go away, so do not get stagnant. Educate yourself and ACT! Leave no stone unturned.
>
> Early intervention DOES make a powerful difference in the long-term progress and surrounding yourself with smart, optimistic, compassionate friends and caregivers makes all the difference in how you adapt to the experience.

Parental involvement in educational planning is a legal mandate under IDEA. Many parents are concerned about their child's progress and need frequent, open, and honest communication from teachers and others working with their child (Stoner et al. 2005). Journals, logs, and point sheets are often used by schools to communicate a child's daily activities. Parents need this kind of frank and direct feedback, because of their child's communication problems. The child may not have the ability to explain his or her day, relay problems and how she or he felt as a result of those, or tell parents what others said or did to make their day pleasant or disturbing. As a result of the child's communication difficulties, parents watch signs and signals in the child's demeanor and behavior, and ask the child questions to get enough information to reconstruct the day's occurrences. The child's inability to communicate well and interpret and convey the actions of others makes parents more reliant on communication from school personnel. Without frank and honest communication that is fairly detailed, parents may feel that school personnel are not being as observant of their child as they should. If parents are not informed of issues, and discover them later, they are more likely to become distrustful of school personnel. Because of the child's disability and the history associated with caring for the child, parents are often more protective and more sensitive to changes in the child's behavior. Changes in behavior are signs of mistreatment, discomfort, and frustration, and these issues must be addressed and resolved to protect and support the child with ASD.

3.1.6 Behavior of the Child with ASD

Here is what some parents say about the behaviors of children with ASD:

> Not all children respond the same way to traditional discipline. What may look like a monumental temper tantrum is really sensory overload.
>
> I wish they could understand that when he is having a tantrum, there is little I can do to stop it other than to be patient and take him out of the situation that is overloading his sensory system; I wish others would be less fearful of the term 'autism'.

According to Fleischmann (2004), children with ASD have angry outbreaks, self-inflicted injuries, lack a sense of danger, overreact to stimuli, and have difficulty sleeping. Myers and colleagues (2009) indicate that children with ASD are difficult to manage, display disruptive behaviors, and create chaos which can make

3.1 Introduction

it difficult to take them out in public. The authors further indicate that behavior problems and emotional issues remain stable over time, which is disheartening for parents of children who are difficult to manage. The explosive and difficult behavior is an attempt to communicate. Children with ASD are unable to manipulate their environment to get their wants and needs met, and this creates frustration that contributes to disruptive behavior. Many are unable to understand what others desire and expect of them, and this creates a situation where they fail to meet expectations. Their failure causes irritation, aggression, and misunderstandings. Still others are very sensitive and changes in their routines create unpredictable situations they cannot control, and their limited flexibility causes them to meltdown. For others, a basic lack of acceptance, inclusion, and respect from others causes them to demonstrate disruptive behavior. Sensory overload can cause aggressive and difficult behavior as well. Too much information can cause discomfort, distortion, and confusion that cannot be communicated effectively, so some individuals 'lose it' because of sensory issues in their environment. As one mother put it, removal from the situation, patience, and waiting for the behavior to run its course is the only thing to do: "Sometimes my child with ASD will act out for seemingly no reason, but there is always a reason. Kids with autism need to be treated with patience, and respect. If my child is acting out, he is not a bad kid. There is something going on in the environment or inside my child's head that is causing him to act out." Sleep disturbances, hunger, fear, and other physiological and psychological problems can also cause an individual with ASD to meltdown. In addition, a chemical imbalance can be responsible for the explosive conduct of an individual with ASD.

3.2 Use of Technology

A fourteen year-old with ASD described technology this way: "It's pretty good!" while another child with ASD said "technology helps kids with things they're not good at, so they can keep practicing" (Ennis-Cole 2011–12). Both are true statements. Technology tools are fascinating, unique, and portable; they support the principles of Universal Design—multiple means of representing information, acting, expressing, and engaging (Domings et al. 2014). Universal design addresses the variability of learners with ASD, allows multiple representations of content material, and supports different learning needs. Technology tools have created more options for intervention planning, learning, and communicating for individuals with ASD. Augmentative and Alternative Communication (AAC), Virtual Therapy or Telemedicine, Video Modeling, Virtual Reality, Robots, Video Games, and the use of technology-created Visual Supports are being used in ASD research and planning.

AAC apps are a powerful example of consumer technology becoming an assistive technology tool. MP$_3$ players and tablets are replacing large, costly, bulky communications devices and desktop computers to provide in the moment, mobile, and customizable support for a variety of needs in ASD: organization, scheduling, communication, directions, visuals, and access to information through email, IM, chats, and the Internet.

Virtual Therapy or Telemedicine is emerging as a vehicle to provide support for families whose geographic distance makes it difficult or impossible to get the services of a behavior analyst, developmental pediatrician, or other specialist (Domings et al. 2014). Video Modeling is emerging as a promising intervention for teaching social skills, demonstrating performance, and helping learners with ASD learn appropriate behaviors and language in group settings (Tartaro and Ratz 2014). The impact of virtual environments on individuals with ASD indicates that transfer, enjoyment, understanding emotions and social interactions is possible (Parsons et al. 2006; Moore et al. 2005; Tartaro and Ratz 2014).

Robots have been used as a means of moving children with ASD from solitary to cooperative social play. The predictable programmable nature of robots improved collaborative behavior in children (Wainer et al. 2010). Video games are enjoyed by many individuals with ASD. There is a small amount of research using this technology as an intervention tool, because it has not been used for instruction; it is more of a solitary activity. Studies have focused on video games as a shared social activity that might promote conversation or social interaction (initiating conversations, maintaining conversations, taking turns, and other procedural tasks). Results have indicated that individuals with ASD can learn to play video games in age appropriate ways that facilitate positive social interaction (Blum-Dimaya et al. 2010).

Parents, caregivers, and teachers should be encouraged by the applications of technology, and they should use computerized tools to create and test visual supports that are customized to meet individual student needs. Visual support can improve academic performance, enhance content knowledge, and support a learner by providing relevant vocabulary. Chapter 4 provides examples of visual support created to facilitate the development of content-area skills in several academic areas, provide background knowledge, and improve the potential for student learning. Chapter 5 provides additional information on applications of technology that are being used to help learners with ASD.

Technology is a wonderful tool that children and adults with ASD can use for edutainment and independent daily functions. However, too much immersion with technology tools might create problems for learners with ASD who demonstrate obsessive tendencies toward technology, develop an overriding preference for the use of computerized tools, and imitate the actions they observe repeatedly in gaming environments. It is very easy to allow an individual with ASD to spend time with technology, if it is available. Caution should be exerted such that content is age appropriate, constructive, and balanced with face-to-face social interaction with others in order to develop social proficiency.

3.3 Summary

Families who have children with ASD have to provide an incredible amount of advocacy and support to their child. They have to constantly monitor the child's behavior and have regular communication with teachers, therapists, and others who work with their child. The child's behavior will be one of the first signs that the child is having a problem, and this is critical, since the child may not be able to communicate his or her situation effectively. Normal activities may be challenging due to the child's sensory perception and level of understanding. In addition, routine activities may be difficult or impossible—eating in a restaurant, going shopping, visiting friends, or taking a vacation. Families of children with ASD are under a great deal of stress, and they may utilize technology to help with academic practice, leisure, scheduling, and other areas.

3.4 Discussions Points

The discussion questions provided below can be used to review the chapter. They are included for reflection, and they provide an opportunity for the reader to test his or her knowledge, and determine whether or not the reader's assertions about families with ASD differ from those presented in this chapter.

1. Is the stress of parents raising children different from that of parents with other special needs children?
2. What are some of the issues of families who have children in the Autism Spectrum?
3. How do parents view their child's future?
4. What can be done to help families who are raising children with ASD?
5. How can technology benefit families who are raising children with ASD?

Chapter 4
Technology-Created Visual Support

Applications Software and Academic Content

4.1 Introduction

Individuals with ASD need additional clarification, detailed explanations, and precise instructions that describe procedures for completing tasks. They may have difficulty remembering how to complete exercises, so written instructions with visual aids can be invaluable learning tools. The use of visual artifacts has been shown to reduce cognitive challenges, social disabilities, and assist users with communication and functional life skills (Hayes et al. 2010). Visual support provides cues that help promote self-regulation, identify tools, provide behavioral support, assist the learner with organization, facilitate transitions, and deliver content (Iovannone et al. 2003). The following examples are instructional aids that support children with ASD as they learn skills in a variety of academic (reading/language arts, mathematics) areas and social contexts. These were created using applications software. Any good word processor, spreadsheet, graphics program, database, puzzle generator, or worksheet generator can be used by parents, caregivers, and other professionals to make instructional aids. It is very important to provide uncluttered visuals. Too much text can cause a visual overload which may prevent the learner from using the instructional aid. It is also important to chunk or organize the material such that it builds skills, presents prerequisite information first, and provides the repetition needed by the learner. Though there are limitations for paper-based visual tools, the examples supplied provide an array of different examples that can be recreated for use in content areas. Prototypes for interactive and intelligent visual schedules are being tested, but those are not readily available and they target language support and time management rather than academic skill development.

4.1.1 Examples of Worksheets Created with Applications Software for Learners with ASD

Children with ASD who are verbal may not understand what constitutes appropriate conversation or to whom they should direct their conversation. The example below was created with Microsoft Office to help children understand the difference between private and public conversations and the appropriate audiences for these conversations. This activity consists of simple circles, names of audience members, and conversation topics. The circles are enlarged and printed in color (one black and one red), and laminated. The table entries are also printed and cut out. During an instructional session, entries from the table are reviewed and the child is asked to place a conversation in the appropriate circle and then add the names of the people with whom those conversations should be held. The entries for the circles should be randomly arranged and the child should practice placing the topic in the right circle (Private or Public) and practice adding the appropriate audience. The red circle indicates something that should not be discussed, while the black circle represents appropriate conversation topics (Fig. 4.1).

This is a visual reminder of inappropriate behavior. Tip 23: Have the child with ASD read these items and explain them. If the child cannot read, read them to the child and discuss them. Demonstrate appropriate behaviors through role playing and videos (Fig. 4.2).

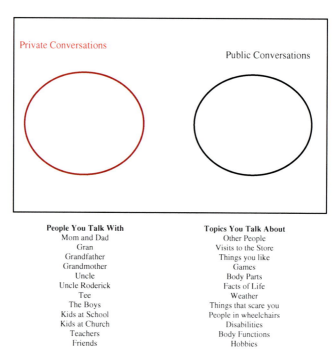

Fig. 4.1 Conversations with appropriate individuals

4.1 Introduction

Bad Things We **Don't Do**:
"BAD GUYS"

1.) **Hitting, Pushing or Hurting People**

2.) **Stealing, Cheating, or Lying**

3.) **Arguing**

4.) **Teasing**

5.) **Talking about inappropriate things (burping or how people look)**

6.) **Using bad words (shut up, idiot)**

7.) **Breaking the rules**

8.) **Being mean**

9.) **Wishing something bad for someone**

10.) **Failing to listen**

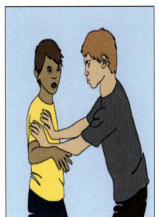

Fig. 4.2 Getting along with others

The use of Comic Strip creation programs on the Internet can help teachers and parents create comics that are direct, simple, colorful, and informative. The example below was created using ComicStripMaker.com to help a child with ASD understand how to treat a friend. Each comic strip conversation can contain multiple tiles, be printed in color, and laminated for continued use (Fig. 4.3).

Character 1:   If you want to have a friend, be a friend.
Character 2:   What do you mean?
Character 1:   Friends don't laugh at each other's mistakes; they don't hurt each other, and they don't grab or pull on each other.
Character 2:   I know that.
Character 1:   I'm glad you know that; just remember that friends treat each other kindly, and they don't hurt each other with their actions or words.
Character 2:   I'll use good words and actions with my friends.

Fig. 4.3 Getting and keeping friends

There are other websites for creating cartoons (i.e., Pixton.com, Pikistrips.com, MakeBeliefsComix.com, chooger.com, toondoo.com, and others). Students can work in small groups to create their own cartoons, and they can use comic strips to tell stories, emphasize social rules, enhance their social skills, promote self-expression, and express their creativity.

Tip 24: In order to facilitate peer support, conversation, and assistance in the classroom, solicit playdates and buddies for the child with ASD. It can be very difficult for children with ASD to 'fit in' and become accepted in a classroom setting. The following is an example of a letter which can be modified, duplicated and sent home to parents (with the consent of the school principal). This letter which follows was created with MS Office Word, and it was used with a child with ASD. Several parents responded positively, offered play dates, and called to learn more about ASD (Fig. 4.4).

Reading is a very complicated activity which involves the recognition of symbols, associating sounds, and assigning meaning. Visual perception is very important in this process. As the eye darts back and forth quickly, cognitive processes are at work decoding, applying rules to unknown words, making associations, and ultimately, interpreting the text and integrating the information into the learner's knowledge-base. Reading is a difficult skill, and many learners with ASD have difficulty with the comprehension component (Chiang and Lin 2007; Whalon et al. 2009). The activities below can help a child with ASD learn to better understand

4.1 Introduction

August 26, 20XX

Dear Parents,

Welcome to another year! We hope you had a great summer filled with fun and relaxation, and we hope your child experiences the excitement of a new school year as s/he learns many wonderful things. We are expecting great things!

Our son, _____, is eager to learn and make new friends this year. _____ is very special to us. He's a very bright little boy who has a lot to offer. He is compassionate and kind, and he is always eager to be of assistance. He has some difficulty with language and social skills as a result of Autism, and we continue to be amazed by his courage and his willingness to try. We are certain that he can learn, if he's given enough time and practice. He is not different from his peers; he gets great pleasure from interacting with other children, and he needs the opportunity to learn play, language, and social skills from his peers. We would greatly appreciate your assistance with this. Please encourage your child to positively interact with him and include him in playground games and activities. He needs other children to talk with him and help him out in social situations; it would mean a lot to him to begin to establish friendships and be accepted as part of the class. He also needs buddies for playground activities, classroom help, and positive role models.

Please help us help him develop play skills, increase his language, and learn appropriate social skills by encouraging your child to positively interact with him.

We think that this would add a wonderful and enjoyable dimension to his school experience, build his confidence, and help him learn lessons for life. It is also a great opportunity for your child to build his/her capacity for tolerance, patience, and kindness.

If you have any questions about Autism or need more information, please feel free to contact us at XXX-XXX-XXXX.
Thank you so much,
The Parents of ___

Fig. 4.4 Letter to parents

words and strengthen his or her ability to decode and comprehend text. Activities in this section cover reading and language arts.

The homophone activity on the next page provides a visual perspective can be used to help the child with ASD better understand words that sound alike, but have different meanings. A *homophone* is a word that is pronounced the same as another word but differs in meaning. The words may be spelled the same, or differently. Video presentations on the Internet on homophones can also be used to further explain homophones (Fig. 4.5).

This activity emphasizes the importance of reading, interpreting, and following step-by-step directions, and it is linked to a character the student might recognize and enjoy. Academic activities can become more interesting when they make use of students' favorite characters, games, and items that are familiar (Fig. 4.6).

Simple visual charts with words syllabicated and used in a sentence can work well for children with ASD. These can be created very easily with applications software. This is a short word list, but more words at the appropriate grade level are ideal for improving retention and the meaning of the words (Fig. 4.7).

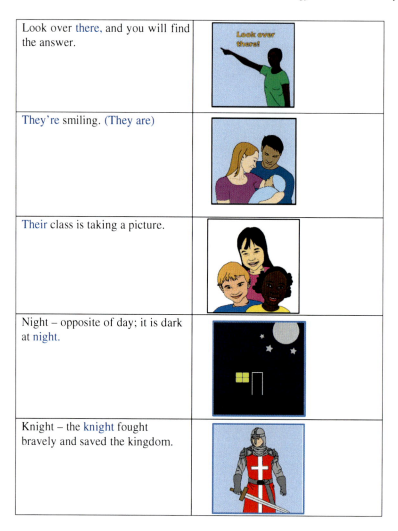

Fig. 4.5 Homophone activity

Puzzles emphasizing readings are a good way to increase repetition of concepts, facts, and useful information. Here is an example from an in-class reading based on the American Folksong "Follow the Drinking Gourd." http://www.followthedrinkinggourd.org/ Video clips available on the web were also used to support this activity. The puzzle has large letters and 15 letters per row; it was created with http://puzzlemaker.com. The student with ASD trying this puzzle found it interesting. He did not complain about the amount of text, and he persisted until he found each of the terms needed. As an extension of this activity, WH questions could be reviewed as well as an exercise on homophones. To make this more interesting and appealing, the actual folksong could be played several times and acted out by the students. Dramatic presentations can help children with ASD learn language, social skills, and content information (Fig. 4.8).

4.1 Introduction   47

Sponge Bob's 2nd Favorite Punch – Orange Fizzle

<u>Directions</u>:
  1.) Circle the <u>utensils</u> (things you use to make something),
  2.) Put a square around all the directions, and
  3.) Look inside your square and draw a line through the action words
  (verbs). These will be words like stir, pour, taste, etc…

<u>Utensils</u>: Get two large spoons, two cups, and two straws.

<u>Ingredients</u>: Things you need to combine to make something new.
  Orange Sherbet and Ginger ale

<u>Instructions for making Orange Fizzle</u>: Scoop out a large spoonful of orange sherbet. Put the orange sherbet in a cup. Pour ginger ale over the sherbet very slowly; stir the mixture until it is smooth. Add a straw, and drink up! Congratulations! You've just made Sponge Bob's second favorite drink.

<u>Reflections</u>:
  1.) What did you make?
  2.) What utensils did you use?
  3.) What ingredients did you use?
  4.) Describe the steps you took to make the drink.

Fig. 4.6 Activity for following directions

Tables for Writing Paragraphs—Often, handwriting is problematic for children with ASD. They do need practice, and as they begin to put their thoughts together for written assignments, the following table can be helpful to keep sentences together, guide paragraph development, assist with spacing, and let the student know how much text is necessary. Dictation software is also an option for students who are unable to produce written work. *Handwriting Without Tears* is one of several products that help make handwriting easier (Fig. 4.9).

This easy exercise can be completed by children with ASD who are beginning to understand the writing process. It includes steps for constructing a paragraph (Fig. 4.10).

Mathematics instruction should be visual and make use of manipulatives. Individuals with ASD must be able to count their money, understand quantities, and apply basic facts. Many individuals with ASD can also engage in advanced mathematical reasoning and problem-solving. Computational ability is a concrete activity that can be a strength in ASD (Baron-Cohen et al. 2007; Jones et al. 2009). When language is applied—word problems, mathematical skills may tend to decline; learners

1.)	possible	Can happen We can fly to the moon, that is possible!	
2.)	Fight	Conflict between people or animals The rams should not fight.	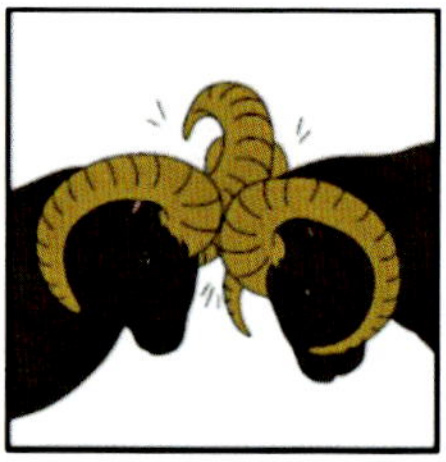
3.)	Knew	To understand or already know I knew those spelling words.	
4.)	friends	People who help and understand each other I have a few friends.	

Fig. 4.7 Spelling word chart

with ASD may find word problems particularly difficulty, because they need to infer meaning from the text and symbols, convert that knowledge into workable problems and apply rules. Many individuals with ASD are good at following steps and procedures, but weaker at making correct inferences and deriving meaning from written and spoken language. A 'translation guide' may be necessary to help the student make better inferences about what operations are needed for mathematical problems.

A legend for symbols and terms is called a 'translation guide.' Charts that clarify language and symbols can help the learner with ASD 'set-up' solutions to mathematics problems and remember operations and rules. Knowing the correct meaning behind the rhetoric can mean the difference between a successful and a frustrating

4.1 Introduction

```
              "Follow the Drinking Gourd"
          N E L G H K S L D U D N W M J
          Y F G S E L N T F O Q P E C T
          M Y T B A K D I I S H T F H G
          T W M V V H U N R O Y H W H W
          M J E U P J K N Z D Y E T C Y
          O R K M H B H C T A C R U T Z
          Y T C M I R D I A S O E E A E
          R S H I A A F A Y N Y R P L S

          F F X E T V E W J N M A V K I
          F O S H I E G G G J F X Z H G
          N B I R Q R Z C O A W P S Y B
          I N R S H Y N Z H B T Z S A L
          K J K I L P D I C W X O E Y H
          P A T C H W G X W Y Q E D B W
          Z J W F T Y U U C V J J V N X
```

BRAVERY - showing courage and no fear
CATCH - using your hands to get something thrown
DRINK – something you do when you're thirsty
LATCH – object that keeps a door or trunk closed
NORTH – a direction that slaves traveled to freedom
PATCH – something that covers an eye
SAID – using words to help others understand you
SLAVERY – treating people as though they are property or things
THEIR – something owned by a group of people
THERE - a place or position
THINK - using you brain to answer a question
WHEN – time something will be done

```
+ + + + + L N + + + + + E + +
+ + + + A + + I + + + T + H +
+ + + V + + + R + + H + H W
+ + E + + + + + D + E T C +
+ R + + + B H C T A C R + T +
Y T + + + R D I A S O E + A +
+ + H + + A + + + N + + + L +
+ + + E T V + + + + + + + +
+ + + H I E + + + + + + + +
+ + I + + R + + + + + + + +
+ N + + + Y + + + + + + + +
K + + + + + + + + + + + + +
P A T C H + + + + + + + + +
+ + + + + + + + + + + + + +
```

Fig. 4.8 Using puzzles

experience. Since learners with ASD have a language deficit, it is necessary to make sure language does not become a barrier to their success. Learners with ASD experience more stress than most individuals, and the natural cognitive dissonance that occurs when learners approach challenging new material can heighten their frustration and anxiety and increase disruptive and non-compliant behavior. Learners with ASD who are repeatedly frustrated will also exhibit negative behaviors if they are pushed beyond their level of competence. If this happens, learning

Name: _____   Date: _____

Writing/Language Arts Exercise

Fig. 4.9 Table for paragraph construction

the content will become a battle, and no one will benefit. Tip 25: Look for words or symbols that can help the learner focus on what is needed. In the following visual examples, key phrases are memorized by the learner. Tables like the ones presented below can be used for both simple and more complex mathematical operations and functions. Ordinary applications software can be used to create simple but effective visual aids that may help children with ASD learn concepts, understand rules, and improve their academic performance (Figs. 4.5 through 4.18).

A spreadsheet program can be used to create multiplication charts, graphs, and formulas that can be dissected and used as teaching tools or supplements to traditional mathematics instruction. The child with ASD may or may not have a propensity toward mathematics, and the instruction will need to be adjusted as necessary. Many great websites can help parents, caregivers, and other professionals enhance the educational experience of children with ASD: TeacherVision.com, ABCteach.com, Do2Learn.com, Edhelper.com, and many others. These sites contain videos, teacher-created visuals, and exercises that can be used to strengthen academic skills. A subscription is required for some of these sites. TouchMath and Signapore Math are other systems which show promise for learners with ASD.

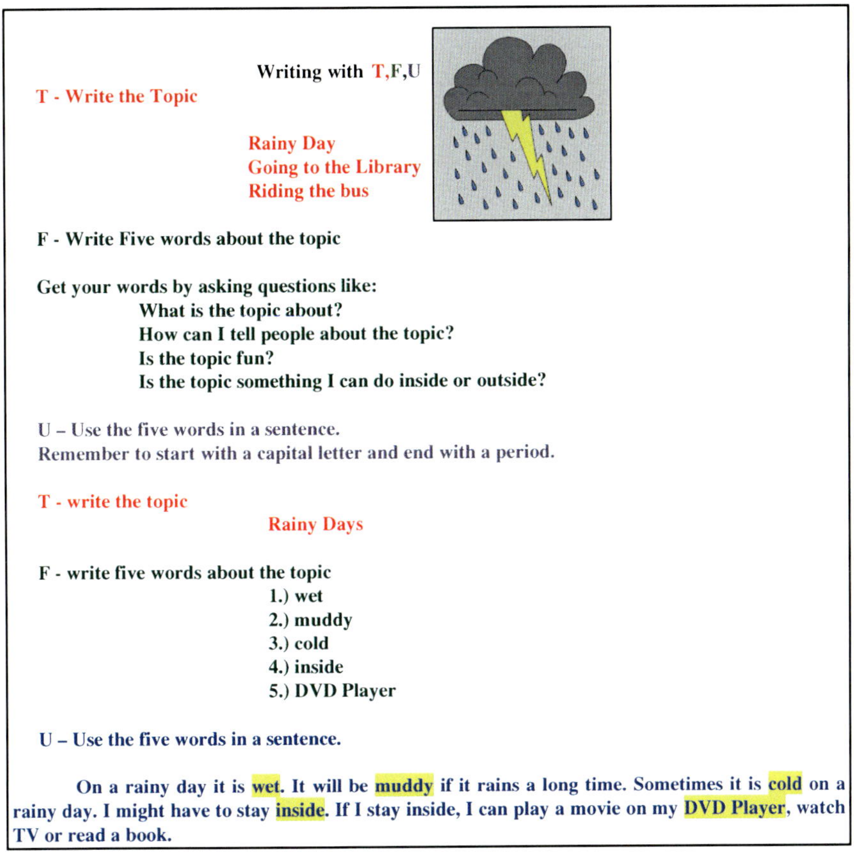

4.1 Introduction

Writing with T,F,U

T - Write the Topic

Rainy Day
Going to the Library
Riding the bus

F - Write Five words about the topic

Get your words by asking questions like:
  What is the topic about?
  How can I tell people about the topic?
  Is the topic fun?
  Is the topic something I can do inside or outside?

U – Use the five words in a sentence.
Remember to start with a capital letter and end with a period.

T - write the topic

  Rainy Days

F - write five words about the topic
  1.) wet
  2.) muddy
  3.) cold
  4.) inside
  5.) DVD Player

U – Use the five words in a sentence.

  On a rainy day it is wet. It will be muddy if it rains a long time. Sometimes it is cold on a rainy day. I might have to stay inside. If I stay inside, I can play a movie on my DVD Player, watch TV or read a book.

Fig. 4.10 Procedure for writing paragraphs

Fig. 4.11 Translation guide for subtraction

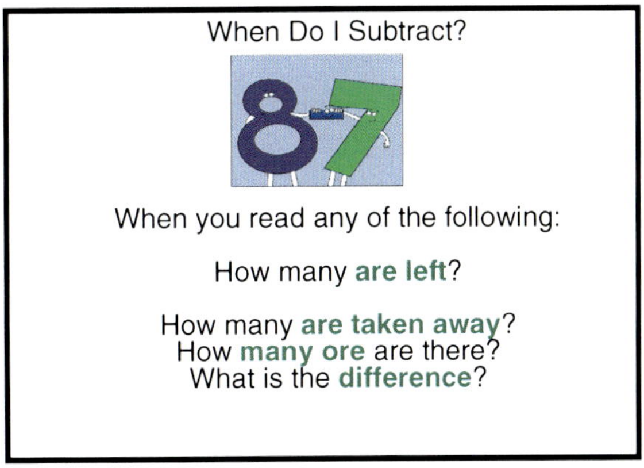

When Do I Subtract?

When you read any of the following:

How many **are left**?

How many **are taken away**?
How **many ore** are there?
What is the **difference**?

Graphs can depict relationships between items. The graph below was created with Microsoft Office Excel, and it helped a learner with ASD explain an experiment on friction. The use of commonly available applications software can be

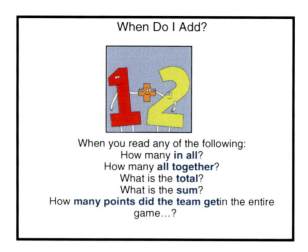

Fig. 4.12 Translation guide for addition

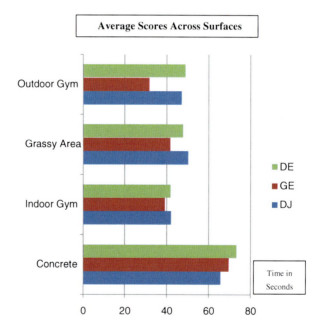

Fig. 4.13 Graph of runners on various surfaces

very helpful to individuals with ASD who are learning academic skills. The visual representations create a comfortable and engaging way to facilitate question and answer sessions and support memory (Fig. 4.13).

Multiplication tables form the basis for advanced mathematics, and children with ASD should have the opportunity to learn these tables. A spreadsheet program can be used to create them, or a tool like hot dots Flash Cards for Multiplication can be used. The Hot Dots set covers division, telling time,

4.1 Introduction

fractions, money, addition, and subtraction. The Hot Dots sets can be used to provide independent math practice. A special pen can be purchased with the set which gives the student feedback during their practice sessions. The pen can provide music as feedback or voice prompts. The multiplication grid below was created with MS Office Excel (Fig. 4.14).

Teach Reciprocal Operations Together—Teach addition and subtraction together and multiplication and division together. An individual with ASD may refuse to learn certain operations, because of a lack of cognitive flexibility, so it is useful to show relationships among operations and other activities. This promotes additional learning and shows a connection that may reduce the learner's anxiety and stress (Fig. 4.15).

Count By:							
TWO	2	4	6	8	10	12	14
THREE	3	6	9	12	15	18	21
FOUR	4	8	12	16	20	24	28
FIVE	5	10	15	20	25	30	35
SIX	6	12	18	24	30	36	42
SEVEN	7	14	21	28	35	42	49
EIGHT	8	16	24	32	40	48	56
NINE	9	18	27	36	45	54	63
TEN	10	20	30	40	50	60	70

Fig. 4.14 Multiplication tables

Multiplication and Divisions are Opposites or Reciprocal Operations

2 x 3 = 6 6÷2 = 3 6÷3 = 2	2 x 9 = 18 18÷2 = 9 18÷9 = 2	2 x 7 = 14 14÷2 = 7 14÷7 = 2
3 x 6 = 18 18÷6 = 3 18÷3 = 6	3 x 9 = 27 27÷9 = 3 27÷3 = 9	3 x 8 = 24 24÷8 = 3 24÷3 = 8
5 x 8 = 40 40÷5 = 8 40÷8 = 5	5 x 6 = 30 30÷5 = 6 30÷6 = 5	

Fig. 4.15 Reciprocal operations

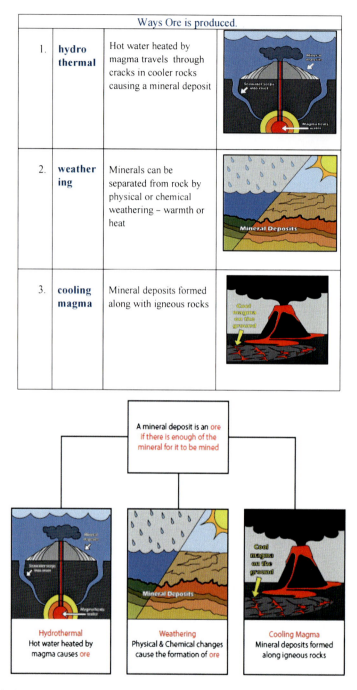

Fig. 4.16 Ore production

4.1 Introduction

Science content can be challenging due to the vocabulary. The successful student with ASD will be one who has had the opportunity to visually understand terms and process their meaning through instructional videos and the following types of charts (Fig. 4.16).

Multiple illustrations of the same concepts may also be helpful. Using charting as a form of review, initial presentation, and advanced organizer helps the student visualize terms and gain the appropriate vocabulary for understanding and applying the terminology.

In the following science example, the student was studying the different forms of hydrocarbons, and the chart presented below was an easy visual which distinguished between the types of hydrocarbons, provided an example of each, and identified uses. Pictures of each—petroleum, natural gas, and asphalt could be included for further explanation (Fig. 4.17).

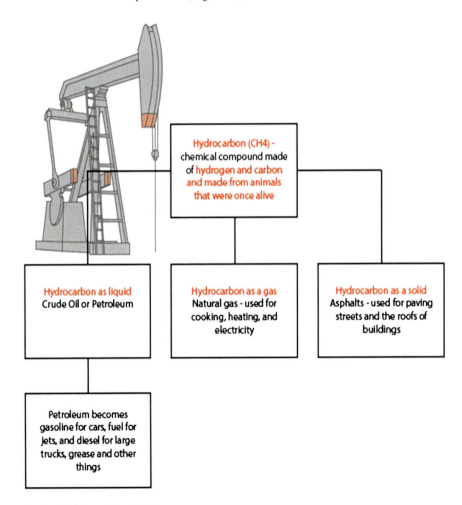

Fig. 4.17 Hydrocarbon (CH_4)

The **Geologic Eras** from Oldest to Youngest:
1. **Paleozoic** – means "old life" The Paleozoic Era occurred 540 million years ago, and lots of fossils have been found from this era

2. **Mesozoic** – means "middle life" The Mesozoic Era occurred 248 million years ago, and **reptiles** dominated the earth.

3. **Cenozoic** – means "new life" The Cenozoic Era occurred 65 million years ago with the extinction (going away) of dinosaurs –

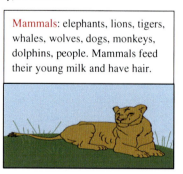

Fig. 4.18 Geologic eras of the earth

4.1 Introduction

This next science example provides a visual representation of geologic eras. The images help clarify time periods and explain terminology (Fig. 4.18).

Visual supports are cognitive tools that help learners with ASD produce language, learn new concepts, and transition between different activities (Bugaj et al. 2014; Hayes et al. 2010). Several forms of support include visual scripts, visual schedules, reminder cards, and visual task analysis (Meadan et al. 2011). Written words and images are paired in visual scripts; these are used to support individuals with social and communication deficits. Visual scripts are recited by a learner in a natural setting and faded (Ganz et al. 2014) over time. Appropriate behaviors and conversation are often modeled through visual scripts (i.e., turn-taking, initiating conversations, requesting items from the environment, getting a break, etc…). Visual schedules provide organizational support; they add structure and predictability for learners with ASD by presenting the sequence of daily activities or tasks. Reminder cards are useful for reviewing correct behavior, language, and interaction with others. A visual task analysis illustrates steps in a process, and reduces the load on working memory by providing procedural information listed as simple steps. Short phrases or single words are paired with illustrations of each step required to successfully complete a task.

Visual support reduces confusion and frustration, provides consistency and predictability, and increases a learner's productivity and independence completing tasks (Newton et al. 2013). PowerPoint Presentations, digital tablets, video, interactive whiteboards, computerized games, and the Internet are tools that can be used in an environment to provide students with ASD visual support. Lessons for learners with ASD should incorporate visuals, because they capitalize on the strengths of learners with ASD. Those include visuospatial skills, sustained attention, associative memory, cued recall, strong focus on details, and graphic comprehension (Quill 1997). An example of incorporating visuals into lessons is Go Vizzle created by Monarch Teaching Technologies. Go Vizzle allows teachers to develop visual lessons easily or use existing lessons created by other teachers. The lessons can be tied to a students' Individualized Education Plan, and used in edit or play mode. Teachers have the ability to use and modify existing lessons in order to more quickly generate individualized visual content to meet the needs of their students. Data on a students' progress is collected, and the results of the analysis are used to make decisions about the students' progress and performance.

Visual support has to be customized to meet the needs of learners with ASD, because there is variability in learner profiles (Quill 1997). Customization can take a little time or a great deal of time depending on the lesson, the creator of the resource, and his or her library of visual images. Internet images can be found rather easily, but those must be cited appropriately. Free graphics and images registered through Creative Commons that permit use are options that can be explored for images. Photographs taken by students are another way to incorporate visuals for instructional content. Images students capture can build interest in content and teach the student additional skills (resizing, cropping, inserting, and optimizing photos, wrapping text for image placement, and other useful skills).

The visuals illustrated in this chapter were simple, and they can be effective tools to convey academic content to learners with ASD. Tip 26: The suggestions below should be considered when visual learning tools are created:

1. print the visuals and allow users to review them often;
2. create visuals with pleasing aesthetics (colors, sizing, and verbiage);
3. use clearly worded text that matches the learner's ability level;
4. use white space often and avoid clutter;
5. balance text and graphics and pair them appropriately;
6. make sure fonts are Arial or San Serif and 12 points or larger (the text and graphics presented in the examples had to fit the template, so those are smaller to fit in the space provided);
7. use vector graphics so that enlarged images retain their integrity when resized;
8. search for and use web-based tools—several examples have been listed in this chapter;
9. provide an opportunity for reflecting on the exercise;
10. use the students' favorite characters, activities, and events;
11. simplify procedures and steps in a process and color code those;
12. highlight key terms;
13. provide short explanations with matching images; and
14. use multiple representations of complex concepts using the same images.

4.1.2 Summary

Charting is a technique that can be used to create simple, easy, and effective visuals for children with ASD; charts can be used for different types of content material, and they can function as an advanced organizer, a review of relevant concepts and terms, and a method for decomposing terms and content to make it more accessible. Charts can be created with ordinary applications software: word processing programs, puzzle makers, worksheet generators, comic strip makers, presentation software, and others.

4.1.3 Discussion Points

The discussion questions provided below encourage review and discussion. Charting as a teaching tool provides opportunities to introduce lessons, review, and scaffold new content to existing knowledge. Review the questions below and add other ideas for using and creating charts.

1. What are three advantages and three disadvantages of charting?
2. How could video-based charts be created and used to further learning?
3. What visual aesthetics make charts effective?

Chapter 5
Technologies to Facilitate Communication, Social Skill Development, Diagnostic Reporting, and Learning

5.1 Introduction

Several forms of technology have been used to create learning opportunities for individuals with ASD. Studies on Video-modeling, AAC (Augmentative and Alternative Communication), Robotics, Virtual Reality, Telepractice/Teletherapy, and Video Games are discussed in the paragraphs below. The review below is not an exhaustive literature review, but it represents a cross section of papers from different disciplines. The literature highlights classic studies that are well-cited, innovate approaches, and studies that show promise as an instructional aid in the areas of communication, behavior, and social skill development.

Video-Modeling (VM) is supported as a promising tool in many studies, and its use has been applied to conversation and play, social communication, social initiation, perspective taking, functional skills related to hygiene, making purchases, following procedures, emotional perception, spontaneous requesting, and other areas (D'Ateno et al. 2003; MacDonald et al. 2005; Nikopoulos and Keenan 2007). Information on VM is listed in the following url: http://autismpdc.fpg.unc.edu/content/video-modeling. Urls were active during the production of this manuscript, but they are dynamic and subject to change. Many individuals with ASD have difficulty communicating and interacting with others, and they are often visual learners, so video-modeling is used to teach them the skills necessary to positively interact with others, request items needed, and engage in social communication. Often poor eye gaze, few verbal initiations, and a lack of pretend and imaginative play are present in children and adults with ASD. VM can be used to address these and other areas of deficit. Based on principles of Bandura's Social Learning Theory, VM allows learners to observe and imitate visual sequences, procedures, and social interactions in order to become more effective at the skills they lack. Learning takes place when the actions and attitudes of respected models are observed and imitated. The model for children is usually a member of their peer group or an adult. Both have been highly effective tools for learning appropriate skills. Observed behaviors and actions are viewed until they are understood, and then those are followed by opportunities to practice in a natural environment to facilitate transfer and evaluate success. Several researchers have examined video self-modeling; comparisons of in vivo and video-modeling have been undertaken in an effort to determine the most effective method. As individuals with ASD watch others perform tasks successfully, the presentation provides the clarity which allows them to observe the behaviors, emotions, sequence of events, and procedures that are necessary.

AAC includes methods of producing speech in an alternative way or supporting language in individuals who are unable to produce speech on their own (Murray and Goldbart 2009). AAC basically supports the production of speech or replaces speech production for individuals who have difficulty generating speech naturally. Examples of AAC: http://www.youtube.com/watch?v=Eb_URYj_L_k and http://www.youtube.com/watch?v=m4OL2bnSv3Q. AAC is used to support individuals who have a variety of medical impairments resulting from dysarthria, apraxia, and aphasia—conditions that affect speech or language production. Dysarthria and apraxia involve problems with the production of speech (retrieving and implementing articulation, motor programming and execution), while aphasia involves problems with language (forming meaningful expression). These conditions are present in a variety of medical conditions including: Cerebral Palsy, Multiple Sclerosis, Parkinson Disease, Traumatic Brain Injury, Strokes, ASD, and others. Individuals with ASD have communications deficits that make AAC a viable tool for learning and producing language. AAC is used to support individuals with ASD who have deficits in expressive, receptive, pragmatic language, and social communication.

Social interaction (sharing, taking turns, social initiation), the delivery of therapy, education, and collaboration have been examined in ASD using robotics technology. Robots used in ASD have been remotely controlled or self-controlled devices with sensors and actuators (Boser et al. 2014). Applications of robotics have been found to be motivating, preferred over human interaction, less stimulating than contact with people, predictable, and valuable for teaching social communication and interaction. Classes designed to teach students to program robots have fostered collaboration, shared problem-solving, joint attention, motor learning and imitation. There are several different robots that have been examined in the literature: CosmoBot, NAO, KASPAR, Aurora, Lego, and others. Examples of NAO, KASPAR, and Cosmobot: http://www.youtube.com/watch?v=_AxErdP0YI8, http://www.youtube.com/watch?v=D6gTHPoO9VI, and http://www.youtube.com/watch?v=wbb6yVC4Lg8. Overall, individuals with ASD appear to enjoy interacting with and discovering the capabilities of robots (Bekele et al. 2012; Boser et al. 2014; Wainer et al. 2010).

Virtual Reality is a created environment where users experience un-programmed, real-time interaction and immersion in either a 3-D simulated or real-world scenario (Riva and Gamberini 2001; Parsons et al. 2014). Users in virtual environments (http://secondlife.com/ and http://www.virtualworldsland.com/) interact in a realistic or imaginary world. Access to this world might involve special equipment (headsets or other head-mounted display, DataGloves, blue rooms) or ordinary input devices. A blue room is an immersive area that a user can stand in. Users can step into and out of the room at will. Inside the room, the user experiences synchronized animation projected on the walls and ceilings. The virtual world is primarily a visual experience, although some environments permit sensory feedback. Virtual reality makes it possible for a user to interact and communicate with others (via text messages, avatars, or verbal input). The realism promotes social dialogue and participation. Virtual reality can be collaborative; this is termed CVE (collaborative virtual environment), and it allows multiple users to enter, meet, and interact with each other through the use of avatars that can take the form of humans, objects, or special characters. Virtual Worlds are a form of CVE, and they have been used by individuals with ASD as a vehicle for promoting shared experiences and dynamic social communication.

Telepractice/Teletherapy is the use of technology to provide access to intervention programming and expertise not readily available due to linguistic or geographic barriers. Applied Behavior Analysis is a well-researched EBI for increasing desirable behavior, reducing problem behavior, teaching new skills, and facilitating the generalization of behaviors across different contexts (Romanczyk and Gillis 2005). ABA programs have to be planned and monitored by credentialed professionals; therapists delivering the programming must be available to work many hours per week. A minimum of 25 hours each week, 12 months of the year are needed for training (Scott and Baldwin 2005). Forty hours a week is not uncommon; the amount of training required is based on the skill set of the individual with ASD. ABA promotes positive and lasting outcomes when it is applied consistently by experienced professionals. It is recommended practice, and it is encouraged for young children diagnosed with ASD; children who receive early intensive behavioral intervention (EIBI) tend to make sustained gains in IQ, academics, language, and behavior (Odom et al. 2003; Romanczyk and Gillis 2005; Simpson 2005). High quality ABA Programming can be expensive and difficult for some families to obtain due to their geographic location, lack of service providers in their areas, and variations in the types of services and support available (Bekele et al. 2012; Gray and Brann 2014).

Telepractice and teletherapy can be viable alternatives to solve these problems. Through telepractice, parents can videotape behaviors and problem situations they have with their children and send those to experts to have them analyzed. Teletherapy is usually incorporated within a broad service plan, and it involves the use of expert advice and parent-implemented solutions for Speech Therapy (http://www.youtube.com/watch?v=w1dON1iYlGU, http://www.youtube.com/watch?v=_-s7LGujKhs), Applied Behavior Analysis (http://www.youtube.com/watch?v=NVK38DIJy3I), and Physical Therapy delivered under the advice and supervision of trained professionals in these areas. This is particularly useful when these types of therapies are not available in the local area.

Video games (MineCraft, Mario Party, PAW Patrol, SimCity) are an entertaining application of technology, and some researchers have applied video game use to social skills learning in ASD. Tartaro and Ratz (2014) indicate that video games can make positive contributions to social group training because they utilize the specialized interests of learners with ASD, they are available for use in many different environments, they promote socially relevant and age-appropriate activities, and they require procedural tasks like following rules and taking turns. The research on social group learning with video games is limited, but several researchers have found that individuals with ASD are capable of learning to play video games, gaining turn-taking skills, initiating dialog, giving compliments, using video games for leisure activities, and exhibiting appropriate play skills (Blum-Dimaya et al. 2010; Ferguson et al. 2013; Gaylord-Ross et al. 1984). Other researchers are providing evidence that video games are being overused by some individuals with ASD in their leisure time, and this is being linked with problematic behavior. This is a danger inherent in the overuse of technology (Mazurek and Wenstrup 2013). Another form of technology, Facilitated Communication, is not recommended for use in ASD, because it was found ineffective (Simpson 2005). These examples highlight the need for evidence-based interventions. Tip 27: Research and evaluate technology tools before using them. Monitor the use of video games to reduce exposure to violence and inappropriate themes. Balance the use of video games and other forms of technology with social activities, chores, educational enrichment, exercise, and other creative pursuits.

5.1.1 Applications of Video-Modeling

Video-Modeling has been used to increase positive social behaviour in individuals with ASD; it has been used to teach a variety of skills: vocational, functional, communication, athletic, emotional regulation, motor skills, and others (Bellini and Akullian 2007). Video-modeling capitalizes on the use of visual presentations; it is learning through observation, and many studies report its effectiveness fostering generalization and maintenance. Generalization is transfer, and that has occurred in both near and far contexts. Dowrick first successfully demonstrated the effectiveness of VM in a variety of settings with children with Spina Bifida, hyperactivity, and developmental disabilities (Bellini and Akullian 2007; Charlop-Christy et al. 2000). Several advantages of VM include its use in natural settings, control over the modelling procedure, repetition, convenience, and consistency. Videos of naturally occurring situations, environments, and actions can be produced. These can be precisely scripted to teach targeted skills by directing the learner's attention to specific events or actions. This is clearly an advantage over in vivo (live) modelling, which cannot be as tightly controlled. The ability to edit video footage allows the producer to remove distractors that may cause a learner with ASD to become overly selective and focus more on distractors and inconsequential elements of the video as opposed to the desired skills. VM scenarios can be observed repeatedly. This allows the learner to view a consistent presentation of repeated skills and actions. Finally, the ability to review allows the presentation to be used with different learners to strengthen their skills. Disadvantages of VM include time for repeated editing and video-taping. Several studies that examine VM are presented below to give the reader additional information on applications of VM in ASD.

Charlop and Milstein (1989) reported that VM was an efficacious tool for teaching conversational speech to 3 boys diagnosed with ASD. The boys were verbal and they could answer simple questions. They had some speech, but they seldom asked questions, spontaneously held, or maintained conversations. In addition, they had a history of being unable to engage in conversational speech through prompting and reinforcement procedures taught by their speech therapists, parents, and others. Both a multiple baseline design across children and within subjects across conversations and a multiple probe across conversations were used to evaluate findings. The videotapes of adults engaging in scripted conversations about toys were created. The adults modelled the turn-taking that occurs in ordinary conversations. Each of the boys acquired conversational speech after participating in the VM procedure. Generalization and maintenance of skills at 15 months post-intervention were reported.

Charlop-Christy et al. (2000) compared the effectiveness of VM with in vivo modelling for teaching developmental skills to 5 children diagnosed with ASD. A multiple baseline design across children and within child across the two conditions (VM and in vivo) was used. Familiar adults were used to model targeted behaviours in both the in vivo and VM conditions. The targeted behaviour was based on the individual needs of the child; those included labelling emotions, playing independently, producing a spontaneous greeting, engaging in conversational speech, performing self-help skills, asking questions, and playing in a cooperative and social manner. After observations of the targeted behaviours were complete, the children were tested for skill acquisition and generalization. The video modelling conditions resulted in faster gains of the targeted skills than in vivo modelling. In addition, VM was cost and time-effective, and it promoted generalization of the skills taught. Generalization was not found in the targeted skills taught through in vivo modelling.

Nikopoulos and Keenan (2007) conducted multiple base line studies where 3 children diagnosed with ASD were taught social initiation, reciprocal play, imitative responses and object-engagement. Videotapes were shown of a child modelling the targeted behaviours, and children were placed in a natural environment where social interaction and communication occurred. Children who watched the VM footage successfully demonstrated social behaviors and social initiation, increased reciprocal play, and decreased isolation.

Delano (2007) conducted a meta-analysis of studies published in peer reviewed journals that evaluated the impact of VM on individuals with ASD. Nineteen studies met the author's inclusion criteria (description of experimental research, manipulation of an independent variable, quantitative measures of a dependent variable, identification of participants with ASD, description of a VM intervention as a primary independent variable, and individualized videotapes created for research participants). Small sample sizes (<4 participants) were recorded in 15 studies, and a total of 55 participants were represented. More than half of the participants were under the age of 8, and three were 20 years old. Skills targeted in the study included perspective-taking questions, challenging behaviours, social-communication, and functional skills. The outcomes reported across the 19 studies indicated that VM interventions were associated with positive gains in the targeted skills; 5 studies provided mixed results. The authors indicated that these may have been attributed to individual participant characteristics: expressive language skills, challenging behaviour, and visual processing issues. Maintenance of skills gained was reported in 14 of the studies; the time line for assessment post-intervention was as little as 2 days and as long as 15 months. Generalization was assessed in 10 studies, and overall, results were promising.

Bellini and Akullian (2007) completed a meta-analysis to examine the effectiveness of VM and VSM interventions for both adolescents and children with ASD. The meta-analysis revealed outcomes from 23 studies designed using single-subject research; reported the outcomes for generalization and maintenance for the studies; and determined whether or not VM interventions met Horner's criteria (2005) for evidence-based practice. Two authors reviewed each of the 29 studies located for inclusion in the review. Eight criteria were used to determine inclusion: identification of ASD in participants; outcomes presented for behavioural functions, social-communication skills, or functional skills; the use of VM or VSM; the use of single-subject research designs; the inclusion of individual data presented graphically, the study's location (a peer-reviewed journal), publication in English, and the absence of dichotomous dependent variables. Six studies were eliminated because they did not meet the inclusion criteria. Inter-rater agreement for features of the studies was 98 %, and PND (percentage of non-overlapping data points) scores were calculated by each coder for each participant and across all dependent variables in 22 of the studies. One study was removed, because individual data points for the intervention were not present. PND scores for maintenance, generalization, and intervention effects indicated that moderate intervention effects were present.

MacDonald et al. (2005) extended the work of D'Ateno et al. (2003) by teaching two children with ASD to engage in long play sequences that used both motor actions and narration. The authors developed play scripts from the actions and conversations of typically developing children playing with three different play sets. The phrases of typically developing children were further developed, videotaped, and used to teach play skills to the two participants in the study. Both boys were diagnosed with PDD-NOS, and both had limited pretend play skills. Both boys had previously experienced video modelling in teaching scenarios, and both had sustained attention during VM. Play scripts were developed for three play sets—a house, ship, and town; each play set required the child to manipulate characters, make verbalizations, and participate in coordinated actions. The children viewed an adult model acting out the sequence of pretend play, and after viewing the VM, the child was given 4 min to play with the material without prompts or reinforcement. Videotapes of the child's performance were scored for scripted verbalizations and scripted play actions. VM was found to be effective for increasing scripted play across the three play conditions. Play chains involved up to 17 actions with verbalizations included; the children learned the scripts in five to seven sessions without experimenter reinforcement. The authors suggest that the type of play in which the children engaged could encourage the development of perspective-taking. Scripted play, along with the actions and verbalizations were observed, but very little unscripted play occurred. The authors indicate that VM is effective for teaching sequences of play, and they encourage more research to develop strategies to increase unscripted and age-appropriate play skills in children with ASD.

5.2 Augmentative and Alternative Communication

Communication is a core deficit in persons with ASD (Beals and Hurewitz 2014). Communication skills are important and complex skills that are often taken for granted. Speech allows individuals to communicate their basic needs, share ideas, express rage, and explain their emotional states. Through speech, individuals understand how to function, learn what needs to be accomplished, and help others get their needs met. The ability to communicate forges social connections and prevents isolation.

Individuals with ASD face extreme challenges in the area of communication. They may have deficits in expressive, receptive, mixed receptive-expressive, and pragmatic language. Persons with expressive language disorder may add words to their vocabulary very slowly, and they may be late talkers. The average 2 year-old uses about 50 words routinely, and the average 2 year-old with ASD does not. The 2 year-old with ASD may make sounds that approximate language and utter some words, but their production of speech lags behind that of their typically developing peers. Children and adults with ASD may have trouble with sentence structure, the use of pronouns (reversal is common), and have difficulty finding words to express themselves. Because they are limited in their ability to use language, they may use more echolalia and have phonological problems. Difficulty with verbal or written expression is common, and there are usually problems creating and using complex sentences. The inability to express one's wants and needs may lead to frustration. That frustration can produce negative behaviour, which is also an attempt at communication. Light et al. (1998) discussed AAC as a means of improving language comprehension and expression for a 6 year-old with ASD whose speech was difficult to understand, telegraphic, and echolalic. His teachers and parents felt that his speech was inadequate, and they reported challenging behaviors (screaming, kicking, pushing and scratching) that were triggered by his frustration with self-expression, and his difficulty working through transitions. With thorough and careful assessment and implementation of AAC, the student made gains in both receptive and expressive communication, improved responses to WH questions, demonstrated the ability to generate meaningful sentences to communicate his needs and wants, and decreased challenging behaviors.

In addition to expressive language problems, individuals with ASD may have receptive problems, or difficulty understanding words, phrases, and concepts like time money, proximity, or relationships. This can make it very difficult to follow directions, respond appropriately, and fully participate in activities. Understanding questions can be a challenge as well as information processing, attending, and listening.

A mixed receptive-expressive delay or disorder indicates that both the expression of language and the ability to understand language are impaired. The inability to convey thoughts and interpret and understand others can make an individual's life very challenging. Verb tense, common slang, and the semantics of language are problems which prevent participation and inclusion.

Pragmatic language involves practical applications of language and its functional use in social settings. Following rules, changing language based on the audience, content, and setting (inside vs. outside voice), using language effectively are examples of pragmatic language. Intonation, gestures, appropriate use of deictic phrases, interaction during conversations, and communicative intent (Beals and Hurewitz 2014) are additional examples. The individual with ASD may say inappropriate things or things that are not related to the conversation or situation. They may produce language with very little variability—in essence, tell the same stories whether or not they are applicable to the situation. They may not know how to join in conversations, make appropriate greetings, request items needed, make demands from their environment, change conversation topics, get the attention of others, or read the body language or facial expressions of others. They may be challenged by communicative intent; not understanding the intentions of others can make them vulnerable to misunderstandings and harm. Software used to supplement Speech/Language Therapy and provide practice with the comprehension and the production of speech include the following: Fast Forward's Language and Language to Reading, Grammar Trainer, Hear Builder's Following Directions, Laureate's First Words, Language Links, and Question Quest, Question Builder's Teach Town, and others (Beals and Hurewitz 2014).

In addition to the problems mentioned above, some individuals with ASD are unable to produce speech do to anatomical problems and structural anomalies like Apert's or craniofacial syndromes. Augmentative and Alternative Communication (AAC) can provide a range of options for supporting or replacing speech for children and adults with ASD. For individuals with expressive, receptive, mixed receptive-expressive, and pragmatic language problems, AAC can support language learning and understanding. For individuals with ASD who are unable to produce speech naturally, AAC can be the vehicle for self-expression. Murray and Goldbart (2009) categorize AAC in the following ways: no-tech, low-tech, light-tech, and high-tech. The no-tech category refers to unaided forms of communication that rely on the body to convey messages. Examples of unaided AAC that require no technology include manual signs, eye-pointing, and gestures. The low-tech, light-tech, and high-tech categories require some sort of aid or tool that is used in conjunction with the user's body to produce communication. Low-tech tools include pencil and paper, communication boards, communication books, photos, and symbols, and they do not require an integrated circuit (Shane et al. 2012). Light-tech AAC include speech output devices that are simple, battery operated and produce single recorded messages. High-tech AAC devices are capable of voice output; these devices are more complex computer systems that produce digitized speech, and they are activated by optical pointers, headsticks, and switches. High-tech AAC devices are portable, and they can be grouped into two categories: dynamic and static display devices. Examples of dynamic display devices include the Dynavox by Mayer-Johnson and TextSpeak Design's Talking Keyboard; these systems have touch screens. When the user makes a selection, the options change and another set of symbols and messages appear. Dynamic devices support larger vocabularies, sentence construction, and communication through multiple channels like email, Facebook, and text messages. Disadvantages include cost and the time needed to program and customize dynamic speech generating devices. Static display devices include the GoTalk Systems by Attainment Company; in these devices, symbols are fixed in a certain format. These systems tend to be replicas of communication boards, and they are limited in the number of symbols and messages they can produce. Selected studies on the impact of AAC and ASD follow.

Millar et al. (2006) conducted a meta-analysis to determine the impact of AAC on children with ASD and other developmental disabilities. The authors identified 23 studies for review that met their inclusion criteria. Of those studies, 6 provided best evidence of the effects of AAC interventions on speech production. Out of those studies, two contained participants with a diagnosis of ASD; one study used Aided AAC with three males diagnosed with ASD and Unaided AAC was used with a male with ASD in the second study. In both cases, positive effects were reported in speech production. Millar et al. (2006) concluded that AAC enhances communicative competence and language and produced modest gains in speech production. The authors indicate that parents and clinicians should introduce AAC interventions without hesitation for individuals with developmental disabilities whose speech production fails to meet their current needs.

AAC intervention studies were reviewed by Balandin (2009), who used 11 criteria for inclusion in the review. A total of 125 participants representing 9 single-subject and two group studies met the inclusion criteria. Outcomes of AAC use indicated that the majority of interventions resulted in modest gains in speech production that varied across participants.

5.3 Robotics

The social challenges, communication problems, repetitive and stereotypical behaviour, executive function problems, and the inability to understand others due to ToM (see Chap. 1) make social interaction extremely difficult for individuals with ASD. Advances in several areas of Artificial Intelligence (Machine Vision, Speech Processing, Neural Networks) have been used to create robots that can function as social agents These devices can be used to educate, motivate, support practice, increase independence, and target weak areas in ASD: eye gaze, joint attention, social skills, language, communication, and motor skills. Robots can be used to improve the outcomes of individuals with ASD.

Eighteen adults with ASD participated in a qualitative study designed to provide insight on their social experiences and the types of support they need to help them feel more socially connected. Semi-structured interviews helped researchers look for major and minor themes. The major themes were activities with a joint focus and shared interests, structured social activities, small group exchanges, and facilitated social support (Müller et al. 2008). Activities that involved group membership based themes of interest to the participants created an atmosphere where individuals with ASD were able to share their passion for their special interest with others who were likeminded. Structured social activities provided sequences of events with a fairly low level of person-to-person interaction. Things like listening to books on tape, watching movies or television were examples. Small group activities worked best in pairs or triads; small numbers of participants helped reduce social anxiety and frustration which stemmed from hyperarousal.

Robots are being programmed with social skills: the ability to recognize others, process speech, use verbal expressions (Natural Language Processing), practice eye-to-eye gaze and social orientation, and recognize gestures and emotions (Bekele et al. 2012). Robots can also track an individual's head, hand, and arm movements. All of these features make them ideal tools for practicing verbal responses, conversation skills, turn-taking, initiation, question and answer sessions, and the pronunciation of words. In addition, studying about robots through design, testing, assembly, and implementation in robotics classes can be used to facilitate social interaction, and help students learn to collaborate effectively and gain knowledge of STEM Fields (Wainer et al. 2010; Yuen et al. 2014).

Robins et al. (2005) reported on a longitudinal study with a humanoid robotic doll (Robota) used over several months with four children with autism. The robotic doll was programmed to act as a dancing toy and a puppet. In dancing toy mode, the robot moved its head, arms, and legs to music. In puppet mode, an investigator moved the robot's appendages or pressed buttons on a laptop to operate the robot. The study was designed to examine the use of the robot as a therapeutic or educational toy which encouraged imitation and social interaction skills. The work was a part of the Aurora Project, and it was based on the literature indicating that individuals with autism benefited from the use of computerized systems and enjoyed using those systems. Video footage of each student's trials was evaluated to determine whether eye gaze, touch, imitation of the robot's movements, and proximity to the robot occurred. Video segmented into 1 s intervals was scored independently by two researchers; the inter-coder reliability was 96 %. Findings indicated that social interaction skills (imitation of movements of body parts, self-correction of movements, child-initiated interaction in the form of turn-taking, comprehending that movement was beyond the robot's ability and moving on as a result) increased. The social interaction skills targeted were role reversal, imitation, and turn-taking. The authors indicated that additional studies are needed to uncover the potential of robots as therapeutic aids for children with ASD.

Bekele et al. (2012) designed a closed-loop adaptive robot-mediated intervention architecture (ARIA) for learners with ASD which embedded a network of coordinated cameras and display monitors that worked with a humanoid robot. The head-tracking provided through ARIA allowed the system to be more flexible and adapt more readily to individual users of the system. Through this more individualized approach, the system generated prompts and reinforcement to help children develop social orienting skills or joint attention. Joint attention was targeted because it is a fundamental skill on which other more complex interactions are based. Without the ability to coordinate and attend to both environmental stimuli and social exchanges with others, language and social skills are greatly impeded. Data from a pilot study using ARIA with twelve participants (6 with ASD and 6 neurotypical children) indicated that both groups of students spent more time looking at the robot than the human therapist. Both groups required more prompting with the robot than with a human therapist. The authors indicate that the findings require more study with a larger sample size for a longer period of time to rule out a novelty effect. They also indicate that the participant dropout rate was 33 %, because the participants needed to wear a hat in order to have their head-tracking data collected. The authors suggest the development of a non-invasive method for remotely measuring head-tracking data. Lastly, the authors suggest that robots could be effective assistants in interventions rather than replacements for humans.

Robots can be very helpful in autism. They can motivate the a learner, encourage attention, serve as an extrinsic reward, collect data on performance and level of interaction, mediate social interaction between the therapist and the individual with ASD, monitor imitation and learning, and serve as an assistant in therapy (Boser et al. 2014; Breazel 2003; Costa et al. 2009). Feil-Seifer and Matarié (2005) define socially assistive robots as a hybrid between assistive robotics and socially interactive robotics (SIR). The goal in SIR is effective interaction with a human being which allows the robot to provide assistance in rehabilitation, education, and convalescence. Children with ASD have found robots appealing; preliminary findings on the use of robots in autism are positive, but further research is needed in this area (Diehl et al. 2012; Iacono et al. 2011; Robins et al. 2005). High costs and the lack of availability limit the use and adoption of robots.

5.4 Virtual Reality

Virtual reality supports practice and role playing in a safe environment where rules can be learned and applied. Parsons and Mitchell (2002) identified important considerations for social skills training using VR: accessibility, ease of use, affordability, repetition of targeted skills, explanations of social skills, role playing, fading prompts, realistic practice, and rote learning for social rules. One important advantage of VR is its support for both behavioural and cognitive approaches to social skills training. Virtual environments are sophisticated and realistic environments that support interaction with objects and people (represented and their avatars). VR has been used successfully in cognitive rehabilitation with learning disabled children, individuals with spinal cord injuries, children with visual impairments, and individuals with motor disabilities and severe handicaps. VR reduces the stress and anxiety inherent in a real world interaction by providing a safe, non-threatening environment where learners are free to explore, communicate, practice, and test assumptions. Parsons and Mitchell (2002), also point out the concerns regarding the use of VR—over reliance on computerized interaction might lead to withdrawal from the real world and lead to obsessive behaviour. The authors dispel these concerns by indicating that virtual environments can be created to be active, less predictable environments in an effort to reduce the possibility of obsessive use. In addition, the authors indicate that VEs should be used collaboratively with others to increase feedback and explanations and practice aspects of ToM.

Preliminary support for the use of VR in the rehabilitation of paediatric disabilities was produced by Parsons et al. (2009). The authors reviewed 34 studies where they examined VR in several areas of paediatric rehabilitation: visual and perceptual impairment, cerebral palsy, fetal alcohol syndrome, attention deficit, and ASD. In four of the five studies on children with ASD, the children were less distracted and spent more time completing tasks, and the VE held their interest. Several studies examined the use of VE for children and adolescents with ASD, and though promising, most applications are exploratory, in the concept stage, or use small sample sizes which limit generalizability. VR is well tolerated, but its ability to help learners transfer the things they learn to the real world is a limitation that is shared by other interventions in ASD (Parsons et al. 2014).

5.5 Telepractice/Teletherapy

Teletherapy, telehealth, and telepractice are methods of receiving healthcare services at a distance. The use of communication technologies equipped with video conferencing, webcams, and Internet access allow individuals in rural areas and those in geographically isolated areas to receive the assistance they need for their child with ASD (Boisvert et al. 2010; Oberleitner et al. 2007). Telehealth based systems can shorten the time needed for a diagnostic assessment, reduce costs, and provide support from well-trained specialists. Many children with ASD are diagnosed in their local school system. In order to qualify for services and become eligible for classroom accommodations and additional services (Speech/Language Therapy, Adaptive Physical Education, Social Skills Groups, Occupational Therapy, and other needed services), children have to be evaluated by professionals in their local school. An evaluation can take months; but the use of telepractice could shorten the process by gathering some documentation the parents could share with the school.

Children with ASD can be a challenge, and their behaviour can be difficult at times. Inappropriate and aberrant behaviours require immediate attention, and parents and other caregivers may be at a loss for handing the situation. If families are in locations where there are only a few Board Certified Behavior Analysts, and shortages of other professionals (Speech Language Pathologists, Special

Educators, Educational Diagnosticians, Occupational Therapists, etc.), assistance could be provided through telepractice. In a qualitative study designed to review telepractice in ASD, 8 studies were located. Seven of those reported successful implementations of telepractice to deliver services for behavioural and diagnostic assessments, behaviour intervention, coaching, and educational consulting. Issues that require attention included ethical considerations for the collection of HIPPA data and informed consent.

5.6 Video Games

Video games can be entertaining, and they can be a good way to increase dexterity and motor coordination. According to Mazurek and Wenstrup (2013), children with ASD spend more of their time watching TV and playing video games (62 %) than engaging in non-screen activities. They spend more hours per day playing video games than their typically developing peers, and they have higher levels of problematic video game use. On average, children with ASD spend 4.5 hours per day watching TV and playing video games and 2.8 hours reading for pleasure, doing homework, spending time with friends, and being physically active. Video games may be preferred because they are predictable, comfortable, easy, and foster a sense of accomplishment or success. Video games can also be used to help children with ASD learn to engage in sports and learn the rules of good sportsmanship (Ferguson et al. 2013).

5.7 Summary

Several forms of technology have been presented in this chapter, and there is strong interest in the use of technology tools in ASD to assist with instructional programming, record-keeping, scheduling, motivating students, serving as reinforcers, and providing the practice needed to learn social and communicative skills. Technology will probably never replace efficacious treatments in ASD, just like it will probably never replace teachers. However, the literature in educational technology strongly suggests that by using different forms of technology, it is possible to support both structured and open-ended models for learning, identify skill deficits, promote fluency, provide opportunities to practice, pace instruction appropriately, help individualize instructional content, support collaboration and research, support visual and hands-on learning, and optimize scarce resources (instructor time, equipment). At this point in time, computerized tools are not a direct intervention for ASD, but they are aids that can provide the engagement and support that help learners with ASD scaffold content in the areas of communication, social skill development, and behaviour.

5.8 Discussion Points

Several forms of technology can be used to support learners with ASD. The discussion questions below are provided to help the reader reflect on the chapter and formulate an opinion about the use of computerized tools and the ways they can support individuals with ASD.

1. What role do you think technology should play in ASD and Why?
2. What forms of technology are being used to address the core deficits in ASD?
3. Discuss the advantages and disadvantages of technology use in ASD?
4. A big criticism of many of the technology-based learning approaches is the lack of transfer. Should we discontinue development because of this?

Chapter 6
The Need for Support, Learning Environments, and Technology Use

6.1 Introduction

This chapter reviews some of the characteristics of learners with ASD that were covered in Chaps. 1 and 2, and adds additional information. It goes on to discuss critical elements needed in learning environments, and it examines technology tools that can be particularly useful for learners with ASD.

6.1.1 Problems in ASD that Require Support

Learners with autism may demonstrate stimulus overselectivity, a lack of generalization, cognitive inflexibility, stereotypic behaviors, communication difficulties, and social skills deficits. See Chaps. 1 and 2 for a more complete description of learners with ASD. Each of these will be described in the paragraphs that follow, along with relevant applications of technology.

Parents who have a child with ASD may think their child has a hearing problem. Quite often the child will ignore what is spoken and not respond when called by name. Sometimes the child may appear to be unengaged or uninterested, but in reality the child may be attending to only one stimulus presented in a learning situation. According to Lovaas and his colleagues (as cited in Paynan 1984), combined auditory (sound), visual (light), and tactile (touch) stimulus presented to children with ASD resulted in a response to only one stimulus condition. When presented with the combined queues, the children with autism were instructed to press a lever, and candy would appear as a reward. Instead of responding to the combined set of queues, the children with autism pressed the lever when only 1 of the 3 stimulus conditions was present. Their responses were different from their neurotypical peers who responded when all three queues were presented; the results also differed from those of their retarded peers, who responded in the presence of 2 stimulus conditions (Koegel 1973; Reynolds et al. 1974). The learners with autism attended to only one part of the learning situation, and this is called stimulus overselectivity. This is also known as tunnel vision; it is not certain why learners with autism have tunnel vision. One theory is that the total picture is very overwhelming, and tunnel vision is a way to avoid overarousal by allowing the individual to focus on a narrow aspect of an object or situation. Another theory is that individuals with ASD are born with a concentrated focus which can be a distraction, so they attend to one aspect of a situation. Learners with ASD can focus on multiple queues simultaneously, if they are presented in close physical proximity to the training stimulus (Anderson and Rincover 1982).

- TIP 28: Be aware that learners with ASD have difficulty focusing on multiple queues at the same time. Structure learning situations which highlight the most important task and avoid distractions. For example, do not ask questions while a learner is engaged in an instructional video. Pause the video segment, gain the student's attention, and then ask the question. To promote transfer of the desired skill, provide opportunities for the student to practice the skill he or she watched. Ask the learner questions and clarify content as needed.

Overselectivity can make it difficult to generalize from one environment to the next. Transfer is the goal of any educational program. We would like to see students learn concepts, principles, and higher-order thinking skills and use those skills in novel contexts (far transfer). When a student is presented with situations they have never encountered, we would like for them to have the ability to take general knowledge and skills they have acquired and apply them to solve problems they have not previously experienced. Overselectivity may make this a problem for learners with autism. Attending to one aspect of a situation or object makes it difficult for a learner to see the overall picture and respond appropriately. It is often said that learners with ASD get lost in the details; they pay attention to specific parts, and miss the whole (or Gestalt).

- TIP 29: Foster generalization by using realistic models, situations, and real world content. Make sure relationships between content are clearly identified, and incorporate visuals often to clarify the skill(s) being taught. Teach problem-solving skills and use those across situations to promote generalization. Example: losing items can be very difficult, but pointing out how to search for items, where to begin, and how to look can help make this easier. Videos can be used to clarify steps, processes, and problem-solving strategies.

Cognitive inflexibility was discussed in Chap. 1; it is the inability to 'shift gears' and work through unexpected consequences, through changes in routines. Unexpected events cause many individuals with ASD great distress. One example of working around this problem is listed below.

- TIP 30: Some learners with ASD find shopping very challenging. The sensory information they receive can become overwhelming or even painful because of the sounds, florescent lighting, number of people, amount of traffic, lengthy travel time, etc. As such, shopping can become a very difficult experience. An unexpected trip to the grocery store after school can be very difficult; transitioning from school to the grocery store might provoke a meltdown. If the trip in unavoidable, provide as much information as possible. Inform the learner with ASD of the change in routine, reassure him or her that the trip will be short, tell him the number of item needed, and take care of any physical needs he or she may have before the trip. Unfortunately, life is full of unexpected occurrences, so it is important to add little differences in the routine to help the child with ASD become more tolerant of change. Vary travel routes, add small changes to procedures, and build on these over time.

Stereotypical Behavior was mentioned in Chap. 1; it is usually displayed when an individual with ASD becomes excited or anxious. The behaviors of a person with ASD may seem odd or strange, but they are a coping mechanism. Replacement behaviors and redirection may help an individual with ASD engage in fewer stereotypical behaviors. Tablets and handheld games may be used to redirect learners with ASD and provide visual and auditory stimulation that may reduce self-stimulatory behavior.

Communication challenges were discussed in Chap. 1, and they will require the assistance of qualified professionals. Communication is vitally important for the child with ASD. Every attempt should be made to develop language skills. Applied Behavior Analysis, Speech Therapy, Sign Language, Picture Exchange Communication System, and other avenues should be pursued with well-trained professionals to see how they can benefit the individual with ASD. Many communication apps are available on the iPad and iPod Touch. These can provide in the moment language support for learners struggling with communication. Adding these tools to a Speech and Language Therapy Program at home and at school could increase interest, support the learner, and provide additional opportunities for language learning (Oberleitner et al. 2006; McConnell 2002). Language skills are needed for social interaction, and often very specific instruction is needed to help the learner with ASD gain social skills.

- TIP 31: Explicit instruction in feelings and emotions, social skills games, and group interaction (social skills groups) may help the learner with ASD explore ideas and concepts from a different vantage point. Role playing and videos combined with explanations may also help the learner begin to notice differences in people and begin to understand the feelings and emotions of others in relationship to their own. Apps such as *Emotion X*, *The Emotion Detective*, and computer software such as *Mind Reading* may also help.

Technological advancements have made it possible for learners with ASD to enjoy a variety of tools to help them practice and improve their academic and social skills. Educational Software (CAI), Assistive Technology Tools, Virtual Environments, video-modeling, mobile technologies (iPads, iPod Touch Systems, iPhone), and electronic games are just a few of the available technology applications that can be used for entertainment, education, and edutainment.

Children with ASD may attend to one stimulus condition at a time, demonstrate problems shifting gears or transitioning, communicate in ineffective or inappropriate ways, and have difficulty interacting socially. Technology tools can provide the repetition, practice, and support needed to help them improve their skills. The engaging and visually appealing nature of technology coupled with learner control, a vast array of tools and resources, a gaming format, adjustable or flexible options, customization, and data collection make technology tools worthy of additional research. See Chap. 5 for more information on AAC, Robotics, and other forms of technology that can be used to support communication and social interaction.

Overselectivity (attending to one stimulus condition) can be overcome by using several queues in close proximity. This is easily achieved in educational games and simulations, handheld games, and the Wii. These types of presentations allow users with ASD to attend to multiple stimuli and focus on a larger portion of the visual learning environment. Games and simulations provide consistent queues, a variety of learning formats, and control over the environment which can combat rigidity and cognitive inflexibility. The learner is placed in a variety of situations and given choices that control various aspects of the presentation: level of performance, game characters, and navigation. This allows the learner to develop more flexible ways of thinking and using the computerized environment. A host of iPad applications for language support are gaining popularity. They are portable, easy-to-use applications that allow users to participate in voice output, sign language, one-touch switch systems for speech, speech-to-text, articulation, and vocabulary building. Demonstrations of appropriate behavior, communication, perspective taking, and social skills can be viewed on laptop computers, iPads, and other devices. Consistent exposure and repetition of desired skills via technology can help the individual with ASD become better at understanding and modeling necessary skills. The child can then practice the skills learned in realistic settings with a guide or coach to facilitate generalization.

6.2 Learning Environments in ASD

A well-organized classroom is needed for student success along with a predictable schedule that helps the student with ASD feel comfortable in the learning environment. The elements of a good setting include comfort, collaboration, choice, and academic accommodation as needed. Since many learners with ASD have sensory issues, the environment should have an ambience that reduces student stress and anxiety. Students should work individually and be paired or placed in triads to engage in group problem solving activities, building projects, and hands-on activities. Students should be active participants in their education; they should have the ability to make some choices of materials, use their interpretations of stories and events, and decide when they take their break.

The teacher should be positive and he or she should assess the learner's strengths and weaknesses before delivering any type of instruction or using any technology. Obtaining an idea of the student's academic, behavioural, and functional levels is important; information from assessments should be used for instructional planning. Curriculum content should be delivered to match the student's ability level. Content can be chunked in a variety of ways so that it is useful, memorable, and relevant. It is not a good idea to outpace a student by presenting content that is above his or her level of competence. Academic content should be individualized so that it pairs the goals of the curriculum with the student's ability. Several different types of accommodations may be needed: shortened assignments, study aids and manipulatives, reduced written tasks or the use of a tablet computer to facilitate writing. The use of speech-to-text software can also be used to facilitate writing, encourage the development of student stories, and note-taking. A Behavior Management Plan may be needed along with extended time on assignments, an assignment notebook or PDA for notes, schedules, homework reminders, repeated reviews, preferential seating based on lighting and/or acoustics, positive reinforcement, visual schedules (manual or computerized), and daily communication between home and school.

Students should receive instruction that fosters a sense of accomplishment. Most students with ASD desire to be successful; they want to have the right answers, and they want to achieve. In order to help them achieve, they need extrinsic rewards. Positive praise, special activities, student selected field trips, game days, technology show-and-tell, time on the computer, and other activities like these motivate students, help them persist through academic challenges, and encourage appropriate behavior. In addition, the learning environment should be paced to match the needs of the student. Students should not be rushed or forced to quickly comprehend information from multiple channels. As an example, rapid-fire questions, asking questions during a video, speech comprehension from simultaneous speakers, writing while reading, and writing while questions are being asked are not good ideas, because the overload of information may cause confusion. Instruction has to be paced to account for speech and language deficits. The curriculum should be accessible, and it should be broken into interrelated concepts that can be used as building blocks for more complicated constructs.

Other ideas for structuring a good learning environment include balancing challenge and success, using technology to add visual and auditory elements that are consistent with the curriculum, encouraging experimentation and hands on work. These practices may help learners persist through lessons; it is also necessary to add motivational elements, because unmotivated learners may create disruptions (Koegel et al. 2010). In addition, lessening the cognitive load, understanding the limits on working memory, team teaching, rotating teachers, strengthening skills involved in executive function (organization, planning, sequencing, etc.), and fostering social competence through examples, group talks, plays and drama, role-playing activities, and small group activities may be beneficial. Iovannone et al. (2003) described core elements that have empirical support and should be included in instructional programs for students with ASD: individual support, systematic instruction, structured learning environments, specialized curriculum content, functional approaches to problem behavior, and family involvement.

6.3 The Use of Technologies in ASD

One of the earliest publications describing the use of computer-based instruction with autistic learners was reported by Colby in 1973 (as cited in Panyan 1984). A total of 13 out of 17 autistic children with limited communication increased voluntary speech following the use of a keyboard and video display. The children had the opportunity to explore and initiate play with the keyboard and video display. Goldenberg and Frost (as cited in Panyan 1984) indicated that autistic learners used Turtle Graphics to successfully control the turtle and manipulate objects. Geoffrion and Goldenberg (1981) found that autistic learners were increasingly more responsive when they explored computer-based systems. While interesting and noteworthy, these early studies provided anecdotal evidence at best. They were not experimental studies with random assignment to either a treatment or control group, nor were they single subject research designs which are also controlled experimental designs.

More studies were conducted on the use of different forms of technology with learners with ASD. The studies provided support for the use of computers as a promising tool for motivating and improving the attention of autistic learners, reducing problem behaviors, increasing speech, and helping learners gain competence in other areas (Chen and Bernard-Opitz, 1993; Hetzroni and Thannous, 2004; Mechling et al. 2009; Panyan et al. 1984; Pleinis and Romanczyk 1983).

With the advent of mobile technologies, teachers, therapists, and parents are buying iPads, iPod Touch, iPhones, and other mobile tools and apps to help children with ASD learn and practice communication, academic and social skills. Mobile tools are being researched for their effectiveness; anecdotal accounts from users indicate that these devices are very motivating, visually appealing, and enjoyable. More research is needed to determine the best practices for technology use with children diagnosed with ASD. The use of technology as an intervention in ASD has come under fire, because of the need for evidence supporting its effectiveness. Too often, fads and "treatments" in ASD have been touted as miracle cures, and they have done more harm than good. They have offered false hope and wasted the time of parents and children with ASD who are desperate for improvement and intervention. According to Knight et al. (2013), evidence for the use of technology as an intervention for teaching academic skills to students with ASD is limited. These researchers echo others who indicate that determining whether or not technology is an evidence-based practice is critical (Gersten et al. 2005; Horner et al. 2005; Pennington 2010; Tincani and Boutot 2005). These opinions are valid, and they should encourage additional research.

The history of the field of Educational Technology involves a very careful study of more than 50 years of applying technology to educational problems, and it supports the following conclusions about the use of technology: no technology can fix an educational problem or supply a universal solution; the use of technology must match an identified need within the curriculum; teachers will always be more important than technology; and just because you can use technology, does not mean that you should use it (Roblyer and Doering 2010). Adopting any form of technology without careful curriculum planning, appropriate teacher and student training, technical support, and a method for evaluation is a recipe for disaster. The integration of technology takes careful planning, assessment, and evaluation. Without these elements, it is impossible to reap sustained benefits. Technology should be matched with the abilities of the learner, and it should add to the learner's educational experience. Learners with ASD can benefit from the use of computerized tools; they can be invaluable for repetition, immediate feedback, practice, visual presentations, performance assessments, collaboration, and adjusting presentations based on the student's ability. In addition, technology can serve as an extrinsic reward, a source of motivation, and an asset when paired with well-planned, guided, and mediated instruction in the skills desired. See Chap. 5 for additional information on various forms of technology.

6.4 Summary

Individuals with ASD have a variety of challenges, and they need a great deal of support that should begin in their formative years. With early intervention, outcomes are better. Challenges attending to one aspect of a situation, cognitive inflexibility, communication, and overselectivity require additional support. Learning environments can be difficult because of these challenges. Structuring the instructional environment with predictable schedules, having qualified teachers who are knowledgeable of ASD and have experience with different learners in the Autism Spectrum are critical elements that foster student success. A variety of different forms of technology can be used to support learners, foster independent learning, practice, and support a visual curriculum. Computerized tools can encourage motivation and provide options for individualizing instructional content.

6.5 Discussion Points

The discussion questions provided should be used for review and reflection.

1. How can teachers support learners with ASD in an instructional setting?
2. Describe the communication challenges that may be present in ASD, and propose two forms of technology that may be helpful for both the learner and the teacher.
3. Explain overselectivity and its implications for instructional delivery.
4. Should technology tools be used in ASD for instructional support or intervention planning? Explain your answer by describing why and how.

Appendix A
Practical Tips for Assisting Learners with ASD

Chapter 1

Tip 1: Get an evaluation from professionals who are using the ADOS and ADI-R.

Tip 2: The use of computer programs and physical activities which expend energy and promote success can help an individual move past a perseverative moment.

Tip 3: Art activities can be used to help develop language, self-confidence, and creativity. Several easy art projects can be integrated into a students' classroom experience.

Tip 4: Simple recorders and machines such as the Caliphone make it possible to listen to sounds, control volume, and repeat as needed.

Tip 5: Presenting uncomfortable sounds in a non-threatening environment and allowing the individual to control the intensity of the sound and the duration can help make ordinary sounds such as a vacuum cleaner, a dryer for clothing, or other household sounds more tolerable. For sounds that may be startling and unpredictable (balloons popping, fire drills, etc.), advanced notice may be necessary along with practiced routines to help the individual get used to the possibility of a startling sound.

Tip 6: Pencil grips, occupational therapy, tablets, and touch screens may be beneficial for students with ASD who struggle with motor activities. Apps like *Dexteria* may help individuals with ASD develop the coordination, strength, motor planning, and the execution necessary to become more proficient at motor activities.

Tip 7: When presenting novel concepts, the vocabulary must be taught first and visually explained as often as possible. As an example, students with ASD studying a unit on rocks should collect rocks, examine them, and look for characteristics.

Tip 8: Consult the National Autism Center (http://www.nationalautismcenter.org/pdf/NAC%20Standards%20Report.pdf) for Evidence Based Interventions, and seek medical assistance from a patient, knowledgeable, and licensed healthcare provider.

Tip 9: In order to support learners, prevent failure and working memory overload, information decomposition strategies should be used to break tasks into smaller components and simplify the information that needs to be remembered.

Tip 10: Learners with ASD have difficulty focusing on multiple visual cues at the same time. Structured learning situations which highlight the most important task and avoid distraction are more successful for learners with ASD.

Tip 11: Instead of asking questions while a learner is engaged in an instructional video or taking notes, pause the video segment, gain the student's attention, and then ask the question. Allow learners with ASD to use a voice recorder or dictation software for notes. To promote transfer of the desired skill, provide opportunities for the student to practice the skill watched. Ask the learner questions and clarify content as needed after the presentation.

Tip 12: The use of a preferred item or the engagement in a preferred activity can educate, entertain, reward, or reinforce good behavior.

Tip 13: Using special interests as a teaching tool is a good strategy. If a learner with ASD loves trains, use trains to teach academic concepts like distance, time, speed, pressure, combustion, movement, and friction.

Chapter 2

Tip 14: Remain patient and keep a low to moderate tone of voice. Realize that the child is having a difficult time, and he or she is not trying to hurt or threaten anyone.

Tip 15: Involve the child's peers in positive and consistent support. They can be a resource for the child and help the child manage in the classroom.

Tip 16: Clearly explaining the task or activity and describing the steps involved, checking for understanding by asking questions and observing responses, and providing sufficient time for interpreting, processing and executing the request are helpful.

Tip 17: Don't say, "Turn your completed assignment in." Instead say, "Put your papers in the orange box on my desk." Don't say, "Let's call it a day." Instead say, "We are finished." Short, simple statements are better than detailed instructions.

Tip 18: Reinforcers should not be overused; they should be changed as the student changes so that they will remain effective.

Tip 19: Time the student with ASD to see how long it takes for him or her to execute a directive.

Tip 20: Do not automatically lower expectations for students with ASD; assume average intelligence, unless documentation is present indicating otherwise. Provide support and 'think outside the box.' Using manipulatives, breaking processes into smaller steps, and demonstrating requirements are beneficial practices.

Chapter 3

Tip 21: Examples of effective practices include the following: preparing the student for transitions or changes in the schedule, using predictable daily routines or schedules prepared in visual or written form, providing breaks, and permitting physical activity throughout the day to lessen anxiety and improve the child's ability to cope with sensory issues that may be aggravated by the environment.

Tip 22: The instructional aid or paraprofessional must be well-trained and he or she must understand the individual student's needs, strengths, and weaknesses.

Chapter 4

Tip 23: Have the child with ASD read items and then explain them.

Tip 24: In order to facilitate peer support, conversation, and assistance in the classroom, solicit playdates and buddies for the child with ASD.

Tip 25: Look for words or symbols that can help the learner focus on what is needed.

Tip 26: The suggestions below should be considered when visual learning tools are created:

1. print the visuals and allow users to review them often;
2. create visuals with pleasing aesthetics (colors, sizing, and verbiage);
3. use clearly worded text that matches the learner's ability level;
4. use white space often and avoid clutter;
5. balance text and graphics and pair them appropriately;
6. make sure fonts are Arial or San Serif and 12 points or larger (the text and graphics presented in the examples had to fit the template, so those are smaller to fit in the space provided);
7. use vector graphics so that enlarged images retain their integrity when resized;
8. search for and use web-based tools—several examples have been listed in this chapter;
9. provide an opportunity for reflecting on the exercise;
10. use the students' favorite characters, activities, and events;
11. simplify procedures and steps in a process and color code those;
12. highlight key terms;
13. provide short explanations with matching images; and
14. use multiple representations of complex concepts using the same images.

Chapter 5

Tip 27: Research and evaluate technology tools before using them. Monitor the use of video games to reduce exposure to violence and inappropriate themes. Balance the use of video games and other forms of technology with social activities, chores, educational enrichment, exercise, and other creative pursuits.

Chapter 6

Tip 28: Be aware that learners with ASD have difficulty focusing on multiple queues at the same time. Structure learning situations to highlight the most important task and avoid distractions.

Tip 29: Foster generalization by using realistic models, situations, and real world content. Make sure relationships between content are clearly identified, and incorporate visuals often to clarify the skill(s) being taught. Teach problem-solving skills and use those across situations to promote generalization.

Tip 30: Some learners with ASD find shopping very challenging. The sensory information they receive can become overwhelming or even painful because of the sounds, florescent lighting, number of people, amount of traffic, lengthy travel time, etc.

Tip 31: Explicit instruction in feelings and emotions, social skills games, and group interaction (social skills groups) may help the learner with ASD explore ideas and concepts from a different vantage point.

Appendix B
Chapter Resources

Chapter 1		
Autodesk sketchbook pro	http://www.autodesk.com/products/sketchbook-pro/overview	Sketching and drawing
ArtTouch	http://www.attainmentcompany.com/arttouch-software	Drawing program with drag and drop stencils
Corel Paint it!	http://www.corel.com/corel/product/index.jsp?pid=prod3750106&cid=catalog50008&segid=1013&storeKey=ca&languageCode=en	Photo processing—turns photos into customizable works of art
Caliphone CAR2020 Card Master Card Reader	https://www.schooloutfitters.com/catalog/product_info/pfam_id/PFAM29523/products_id/PRO41158	Sound sensitization, pronunciations of word sounds, student and teacher recordings
	http://www.specialed.us/autism/assist/asst14.htm	
Dexteria	https://itunes.apple.com/us/app/dexteria-fine-motor-skill/id420464455?mt=8	Targets fine motor skill development which is needed for written work
Dragon Dictate	http://www.nuancemobilelife.com/apps/dragon-dictation/	Speech to text software
DrawPlus X6	http://www.serif.com/drawplus/	Software for graphic design
Dynavox	http://www.dynavoxtech.com/default.aspx?s_kwcid=TC|16134|dynavox||S|e|15960397390&gclid=CKaszb2Oh78CFTJo7AodKUEAGQ	AAC Device
FaceLand	http://www.do2learn.com/subscription/do2learn_plus/faceland.php	Practicing recognizing and understanding emotions

Chapter 1

Google SketchUp	http://www.sketchup.com/?gclid=CLKV9IGPh78CFWrl7Aod1WQAz	Creation of 3D renderings
Mind Reading	http://www.jkp.com/mindreading/	Extensive library for learning emotions displayed by a variety of age groups
Minecraft National Autism Center	https://minecraft.net/ http://www.nationalautismcenter.org/pdf/NAC%20Standards%20Reports.pdf	Game for solidary or group play—users build structures and create worlds
SimCity	https://www.origin.com/en-us/store/buy/simcity-2013-/mac-pc-download/base-game/standard-edition?utm_campaign=origin-search-us-pbm-g-sim13-e&utm_medium=cpc&utm_source=google&utm_term=simcity%205&sourceid=origin-search-us-pbm-g-sim13-e	Simulation game for building cities and making choices
Lego starwars	http://education.lego.com/en-us	Robotics, video games, STEM focus
Super Mario Brothers	http://mario.nintendo.com/	Reinforcing appropriate behavior, motor skill development, leisure, initiating and maintaining social interaction through game play
The emotion detective	https://itunes.apple.com/us/app/emotion-detective/id523056642?mt=8	App to support the recognition of emotions
Transporters	http://www.thetransporters.com/	Video to support the recognition of emotions
Xara photo and graphic designer 9	http://www.xara.com/us/graphics/xara-photo-editing-software/?gclid=CIeZ_PeTh78CFc9j7AodT38A0Q	Photo editing and graphic design

Chapter 2

Autism speaks' ITA	http://www.autismspeaks.org/science/innovative-technology	Innovative technology for autism initiative
CASST	http://www.coping.us/images/Sansosti_Powell_2008_Social_Stories_Comm_Skills.pdf	The Use of computer-assisted social stories to improve social functions
CAT/CAI	http://www.researchautism.net/publications/4543/use-of-computer-assisted-technologies-(cat)-to-enhance-social,-communicative,-and-language-development-in-children-with-autism-spectrum-disorders	Results of the use of computer-assisted training or computer assisted-instruction

Appendix B: Chapter Resources

Chapter 2		
IAN community	http://www.iancommunity.org/	Interactive autism network
Social stories	http://www.thegraycenter.org/social-stories	Manual or computerized stories used to teach, identify changes in routines, and help students understand unfamiliar places and processes

Chapter 4		
ABCTeach	http://www.abcteach.com/	Printable worksheet exercises and activities
CLASS	Community Living Assistance and Support Services in TX (Check your local Dept. of Aging and Disability Services) http://www.dads.state.tx.us/providers/CLASS/choicelist/index.html	Support for individuals with disabilities
Chogger	http://chogger.com/creator	Comic strip creator
Creative commons	http://search.creativecommons.org/	Public domain images for worksheets and activities
Do2Learn	http://www.do2learn.com/	Educational resources, games, and tools for special needs
Edhelper	http://edhelper.com/	Worksheets and activities for educational purposes
Go Vizzle	http://govizzle.com/	Visual Learning tied to IEPs, progress reports, and student needs
Handwriting without tears	http://www.hwtears.com/hwt	Developing handwriting skills
HotDots flashcards	http://www.educationalinsights.com/category/id/120004.do?gclid=CKWB5LKjh78CFUIQ7AodiF8AOg	Flashcards and pens for individual review, drill, and practice—math facts, time, money, and other instructional areas
Interactive whiteboards	https://smarttech.com/Solutions/Education+Solutions/Products+for+education/Interactive+whiteboards+and+displays/SMART+Board+interactive+whiteboards	Large touch screen that combine the traditional whiteboard with the power of a computer to produce interactive visual instruction
MakeBeliefsComix	http://www.makebeliefscomix.com/Comix/	Comic strip maker
MicroSoft office suite	http://office.microsoft.com/en-us/buy-microsoft-office-professional-2013-FX102918381.aspx	Word, powerpoint, excel, access

Chapter 4		
Pixton	http://www.pixton.com/	Comic strip program
PuzzleMaker	http://puzzlemaker.com	Making puzzles
Signapore math	http://www.singaporemath.com/	Math instruction
TouchMath	https://www.touchmath.com/	Math instruction

Chapter 6		
FaceMaze	https://web.uvic.ca/~carte/research.html	Game for increasing social recognition in individuals with ASD
Fast forward's language and language to read	http://www.scilearn.com/products/fast-forword-language-series/	Reading and language practice and support
GoTalk systems	http://www.bindependent.com/gotalk.htm	AAC Devices to support language and communication
Grammar trainer	http://autism-language-therapies.com/	Visual grammar exercises
Hear builder's following directions	http://www.hearbuilder.com/	Strengthening and practicing comprehension, listening, and following directions
	http://www.superduperinc.com/products/view.aspx?stid=575#.U6OTMthOWdI	
Laureate's first words and language links	http://www.laureatelearning.com/	Functional and social communication
Question builder's teach town	http://www.difflearn.com/product/TeachTown_Social_Skills_Curriculum_Vol_1/video_modeling	Social skill development
SecondLife	http://secondlife.com/?gclid=CMvtgbmvh78CFQMT7Aod1CsA5g	Virtual World - leisure, communication with others, non-threatening social environment for learning
Textspeak design's talking keyboard	http://www.textspeak.com/talktype.htm	Converts typed text into speech for non-verbal or language impaired individuals

References

Alloway, T. P., Rajendran, G., & Archibald, L. (2009). Working memory in children with developmental disorders. *Journal of Learning Disabilities, 42*(4), 372–382. doi:10.1177/0022219409335214.

Anderson, N., & Rincover, A. (1982). The generality of overselectivity in developmentally disabled children. *Journal of Experimental Psychology, 34*(2), 217–230. doi:10.1016/0022-0965(82)90043-1.

Ashburner, J., Ziviani, J., & Rodger, S. (2010). Surviving in the mainstream: Capacity of children with autism spectrum disorders to perform academically and regulate their emotions and behavior at school. *Research in Autism Spectrum Disorders, 4*(1), 18–27. doi:10.1016/j.rasd.2009.07.002.

Auger, R. (2013). Autism spectrum disorders: A research review for school counselors. *Professional School Counseling, 16*(4), 256–268.

Autism Epicenter. (2008–2011). History of autism. Retrieved from http://www.autismepicenter.com/history-of-autism.shtml.

Autism Society of America (2014). Autism prevalence rates increase according to CDC, Autism Society responds. Retrieved from http://www.autism-society.org/press-releases/autism-prevalence-rates-increase-according-to-cdc-autism-society-responds/.

Baddeley, A. D. (2000). The episodic buffer: A new component of working memory? *Trends in Cognitive Sciences, 4*(11), 417–423.

Bägenholm, A., & Gillberg, C. (1991). Psychosocial effects on siblings of children with autism and mental retardation: A population-based study. *Journal of Mental Deficiency Research, 35*, 291–307. doi:10.1177/108835760832997.

Balandin, S. (2009). AAC intervention does not hinder natural speech production for children with autism, but natural speech gains tend to be small. *Evidence-based Communication Assessment and Intervention, 3*(1), 11–14. doi:10.1080/17489530902781772.

Baltruschat, L., Hasselhorn, M., Tarbox, J., Dixon, D., Najdowski, A., Mulllins, R., et al. (2011). Addressing working memory in children with Autism through behavioral intervention. *Research in Autism Spectrum Disorders., 5*(1), 267–276. doi:10.1016/j.rasd.2010.04.008.

Banda, D., & Kubina, R. (2010). Increasing academic compliance with mathematics tasks using the high-preference strategy with a student with Autism. *Preventing School Failure, 54*(2), 81–85.

Barakova, E., Gillessen, J., & Fejis, L. (2009). Social training of autistic children with interactive intelligent agents. *Journal of Integrative Neuroscience, 8*(1), 23–34.

Baron-Cohen, S. (1995). *Mindblindness: An essay on autism and theory of mind*. Cambridge, MA: MIT Press/Bradford Books.

Baron-Cohen, S. (2008). Theories of the autistic mind. *The Psychologist, 21*(2), 112–116.

Baron-Cohen, S., Wheelwright, S., Burtenshaw, A., & Hobson, E. (2007). Mathematical talent is linked to Autism. *Human Nature, 18*(2), 125–131. doi:10.1007/s12110-007-9014-0.

Baron-Cohen, S., Wheelwright, S., Skinner, R., Martin, J., & Clubley, E. (2001). The Autism-Spectrum Quotient (AQ): Evidence from Asperger syndrome/high functioning autism, males and females, scientists and mathematicians. *Journal of Autism and Developmental Disorders, 31*(1), 5–15. doi:10.1023/A:1005653411471.

Beals, K., & Hurewitz, F. (2014). Language software for teaching semantics, grammar, and pragmatics to students with Autism. In K. Boser, M. Goodwin, & S. Wayland (Eds.), *Technology tools for students with autism* (pp. 107–123). Baltimore, MD: Paul H. Brookes Publishing Co.

Bekele, E., Lahiri, U., Sawson, A., Crittendon, J., Warren, Z., & Sarkar, N. (2012). A step towards developing adaptive robot-mediated intervention architecture (ARIA) for children with autism. *IEEE Transactions of Neural Systems and Rehabilitation Engineering, 21*(2), 289–299. doi:10.1109/TNSRE.2012.2230188.

Bellini, S., & Akullian, J. (2007). A meta-analysis of video modeling and video self-modeling interventions for children and adolescents with autism spectrum disorders. *Exceptional Children, 73*(3), 264–287.

Bennetto, L., Pennington, B., & Rogers, S. (1996). Intact and impaired memory functions in Autism. *Child Development, 67*(4), 1816–1835. doi:10.1111/j.1467-8624.1996.tb01830.x.

Blum-Dimaya, A., Reeve, S., Reeve, K., & Hoch, H. (2010). Teaching children with autism to play a video game using activity schedules and game-embedded simultaneous video modeling. *Education and Treatment of Children, 33*(3), 351–371.

Boisvert, M., Lang, R., Andrianopoulos, M., & Boscardin, M. (2010). Telepractice in the assessment and treatment of individuals with autism spectrum disorders: A systematic review. *Developmental Neurorehabilitation, 13*(6), 423–432. doi:10.3109/17518423.2010.499889.

Bölte, S., Goland, O., Goodwin, M., & Zwaigenbaum, L. (2010). Editorial: What can innovative technolgies do for Autism Spectrum Disorders. *Autism, 14*(3), 155–159. doi:10.1177/1362361310365028.

Boser, K., Lathan, C., Safos, C., Shewbridge, R., Samango-Sprouse, C., & Michalowski, M. (2014). Using therapeutic robots to teach studens with autism in the classroom. In K. Boser, M. Goodwin, & S. Wayland (Eds.), *Technology Tools for Students with Autism* (pp. 85–104). Baltimore, MD: Paul H. Brookes Publishing Co.

Boyd, B., Conroy, M., Mancil, G., Nakao, T., & Alter, P. (2007). Effects of circumscribed interests on the social behaviors of children with Autism Spectrum Disorders. *Journal of Autism and Developmental Disorders, 37*(8), 1550–1561. doi:10.1007/s10803-006-0286-8.

Boyd, B., McDonough, S., & Bodfish, J. (2012). Evidence-based behavioral interventions for repetitive behaviors in Autism. *Journal of Autism and Developmental Disorders, 42*(6), 1236–1248. doi:10.1007/s10803-011-1248-z.

Breazel, C. (2003). Toward sociable robots. *Robotics and Autonomous Systems, 42*(3-4), 167–175. doi:10.1016/S0921-8890(02)00373-1.

Bregman, J. (2005). Definitions and characteristics of the Spectrum. In D. Zager (Ed.), *Autism spectrum disorders identification, education, and treatment* (3rd ed., pp. 3–46). Mahwah, NJ: Lawrence Erlbaum Associates.

Brewin, B. J., Renwick, R., & Schormans, A. F. (2008). Parental perspectives of the quality of life in school environments for children with Asperger Syndrome. *Focus on Autism and Other Development Disabilities, 23*(4), 242–252. doi:10.1177/1088357608322997.

Brown, H., Oram-Cardy, J., & Johnson, A. (2013). A meta-analysis of the reading comprehension skills of individuals on the Autism Spectrum. *Journal of Autism and Developmental Disorders, 43*(4), 932–955. doi:10.1007/s10803-012-1638-1.

Bugaj, C., Hartman, M., & Nichols, M. (2014). Classroom-based technology tools. In K. Boser, M. Goodwin, & S. Wayland (Eds.), *Technology tools for students with autism: Innovations that enhance independence and learning* (pp. 47–62). Baltimore, MD: Paul H. Brookes Publishing Co.

Calhoun, J. (2006). Executive functions: A discussion of the issues facing children with autism spectrum disorders and related disorders. *Seminars in Speech and Language, 27*(1), 60–71.

References

Center for Disease Control and Prevention. (2010). Autism spectrum disorders (ASDs). Retrieved from http://www.cdc.gov/ncbddd/autism/data.html.

Charlop-Christy, M., Le, L., & Freeman, K. (2000). A comparison of video modeling with in vivo modeling for teaching children with Autism. *Journal of Autism and Developmental Disorders, 30*(6), 537–552. doi:10.1023/A:1005635326276.

Charlop, M., & Milstein, J. (1989). Teaching autistic children conversational speech using video modeling. *Journal of Applied Behavior Analysis, 22*(3), 275–285. doi:10.1901/jaba.1989.22-275.

Chen, S. A., & Bernard-Opitz, V. (1993). Comparison of personal and computer-assisted instruction for children with Autism. *Mental Retardation, 31*(6), 368–376.

Chiang, H., & Lin, Y. (2007). Reading comprehension instruction for students with Autism Spectrum Disorders: A review of the literature. *Focus on Autism and Other Developmental Disabilities, 22*(4), 259–267. doi:10.1177/10883576070220040801.

Clark, R., & Choi, S. (2005). Five design principles for experiments on the effects of animated pedagogical agents. *Journal of Educational Computing Research, 32*(3), 209–225. doi:10.2190/7LRM-3BR2-44GW-9QQY.

Costa, S., Resende, J., Soares, F., Ferreira, M., Santos, C., Moreira, F. (2009). Applications of simple robots to encourage social receptiveness of adolescents with autism. Conference Proceedings: *Annual International Conference of the IEEE on Engineering in Medicine and Biology Society,* 5072–5075. doi: 10.1109/IEMBS.2009.5334269.

Cox, N., Reeve, R., Cox, S., & Cox, D. (2008). Brief report: Driving and young adults with ASD: Parents' experiences. *Journal of Autism and Developmental Disorders, 42*(10), 2257–2262. doi:10.1007/s10803-12-1470-7.

CTGV. (1990). Anchored instruction and its relationship to situated cognition. *Educational Researcher, 19*(6), 2–10.

D'Ateno, P., Magiapanello, K., & Taylor, B. (2003). Using video modeling to teach complex play sequences to a preschooler with autism. *Journal of Positive Behavior Interventions, 5*(1), 5–11. doi:10.1177/10983007030050010801.

Delano, M. (2007). Video Modeling Interventions for Individuals with Autism. *Remedial and Special Education, 28*(1), 33–42. doi:10.1177/07419325070280010401.

Diehl, J., Schmitt, L., Villano, M., & Crowell, C. (2012). The clinical use of robots for individuals with autism spectrum disorders: A critical review. *Research in Autism Spectrum Disorders, 6*(1), 249–262. doi:10.1016/j.rasd.2011.05.006.

Domings, Y., Crevecoeur, Y., & Ralabate, P. (2014). Universal design for learning: Meeting the needs of learners with autism spectrum disorders. In K. Boser, M. Goodwin, & S. Wayland (Eds.), *Technology tools for students with autism* (pp. 21–41). Baltimore, MD: Paul H. Brookes Publishing Co.

Dunlap, G., Robbins, F., & Darrow, M. (1994). Parents' reports of their children's challenging behaviors: Results of a statewide survey. *Mental Retardation, 32*(3), 206–212.

Durand, V. (2005). Past, present, and emerging directions in education. In D. Zager (Ed.), *Autism spectrum disorders identification, education, & treatment* (3rd ed., pp. 89–109). Mahwah, NJ: Lawrence Erlbaum Associates.

Ennis, W, Jr. (2012). *Simple art: Creative art activities for children.* Pittsburgh, PA: RoseDog Books.

Ennis-Cole, D. (Nov. 2011–Jan. 2012). Teaching students with ASD: Technology, curriculum, and common sense. *i-manager's Journal on Educational Psychology, 5*(3), 52–61.

Ennis-Cole, D., Durodoye, B., & Harris, H. (2013). The impact of culture on autism diagnosis and treatment: Considerations for counselors and other professionals. *The Family Journal: Counseling and Therapy for Couples and Families, 21*(3), 279–287. doi:10.1177/1066480713476834.

Estes, A., River, V., Bryan, M., Cali, P., Dawson, G. (2011). Discrepancies between academic achievement and intellectual ability in higher-functioning school-aged children with autism spectrum disorder. *Journal of Autism and Developmental Disorders, 41*(8), 1044–1052. doi:10.1007/s10803-010-1127-3.

Feil-Seifer, D., & Matarié, M. (2005). Defining socially assistive robotics. *Annual International Conference of the IEEE on Rehabilitation Robotics, 465*–468. doi: 10.1109/ICORR.2005.1501143.

Ferguson, B., Gillis, J., & Sevlever, M. (2013). A brief group intervention using video games to teach sportsmanship skills to children with Autism Spectrum Disorders. *Child & Family Behavior Therapy, 35*(4), 293–306. doi: http://dx.doi.org/10.1080/07317107.2013.846648.

Fisman, S., Wolf, L., Ellison, D., Gillis, B., & Freeman, T. (2000). A longitudinal study of siblings of children with chronic disabilities. *Canadian Journal of Psychiatry, 45*(4), 369–375.

Fleischmann, A. (2004). Narratives published on the Internet by parents of children with Autism: What do they reveal and why is it important? *Focus on Autism and Other Developmental Disabilities, 19*(1), 35–43. doi:10.1177/10883576040190010501.

Foxx, R. M., & Azrin, N. H. (1973). The elimination of autistic self-stimulatory behavior by overcorrection. *Journal of Applied Behavior Analysis, 6*(1), 1–14. doi:10.1901/jaba.1973.6-1.

Frith, U. (2001). Mind blindness and the brain in autism. *Neuron, 32*, 969–979.

Ganz, J., Boles, M., Goodwyn, F., & Flores, M. (2014). Efficacy of handheld electronic visual supports to enhance vocabulary in children with ASD. *Focus on Autism and Other Developmental Disabilities, 29*(1), 3–12. doi:10.1177/1088357613504991.

Gaylord-Ross, R., Haring, T., Breen, C., & Pitts-Conway, V. (1984). The training and generalization of social interaction skills with Autistic youth. *Journal of Applied Behavior Analysis, 17*(2), 229–247. doi:10.1901/jaba.1984.17-229.

Geoffrion, L., & Goldernberg, E. (1981). Computer-based learning systems for communication-handicapped children. *Journal of Special Education, 15*(3), 325–332. doi:10.1177/002246698101500303.

Gersten, R., Fuchs, L. S., Compton, D., Coyne, M., Greenwood, C., & Innocenti, M. S. (2005). Quality indicators for group experimental and quasi-experimental research in special education. *Exceptional Children, 71*(2), 149–164.

Goldstein, E. B. (2011). *Cognitive Psychology: Connecting Mind, Research, and Everyday Experience*, 3rd. ed. Belmont, CA: Wadsworth.

Goodwin, M. S. (2008). Enhancing and accelerating the pace of autism research and treatment. *Focus on Autism and Other Developmental Disabilities, 23*(2), 125–128. doi:10.1177/1088357608316678.

Grandin, T., & Duffy, K. (2008). *Developing talents: Careers for individuals with Asperger Syndrome and High-Functioning Autism*. (pp. 6–19). Shawnee Mission, KS: Autism Asperger Publishing.

Gray, D. (2006). Coping over time: the parents of children with Autism. *Journal of Intellectual Disability Research, 50*, 970–976. Retrieved from http://www.autismtruths.org/pdf/6.%20Coping%20over%20time%20the%20parents%20of%20children%20with%20autism-Journal%20of%20Intellectual%20Disability%20Research.pdf.

Gray, T., & Brann, A. (2014). What is driving innovative and assistive technology solutions in autism services? In K. Boser, M. Goodwin, & S. Wayland (Eds.), *Technology tools for students with autism* (pp. 3–19). Baltimore, MD: Paul H. Brookes Publishing Co.

Greenaway, R., & Howlin, P. (2010). Dysfunctional attitudes and perfectionism and their relationship to anxious and depressive symptoms in boys with Autism Spectrum Disorders. *Journal of Autism and Developmental Disorders, 40*(10), 1179–1187. doi:10.1007/s10803-010-0977-z.

Griswold, D. E., Barnhill, G. P., Smith Myles, B. S., Hagiwara, T., & Simpson, R. L. (2002). Asperger Syndrome and academic achievement. *Focus on Autism and Other Developmental Disabilities, 17*(2), 94–102. doi:10.1177/10883576020170020401.

Grossi, D., Marcone, R., Cinquegrana, T., & Gallucci, M. (2013). On the differential nature of induced and incidental echolalia in Autism. *Journal of Intellectual Disability Research, 57*(10), 903–912. doi:10.1111/j.1365-2788.2012.01579.x.

Happé, F., & Vital, P. (2009). What aspects of Autism predispose to talent? *Philosophical Transactions of the Royal Society of London Series B: Biological Sciences, 364*, 1369–1375. doi:10.1098/rstb.2008.0332.

References

Hayes, G., Hirano, S., Marcu, G., Monibi, M., Nguyen, D., & Yeganyan, M. (2010). Interactive visual supports for children with autism. *Personal and Ubiquitous Computing, 14*, 663–683. doi:10.1007/s00779-010-0294-8.

Hermelin, B., & O'Cononr, N. (1967). Remembering of words by psychotic and subnormal children. *British Journal of Psychology, 58*(3–4), 213–218. doi:10.1111/j.2044-8295.1967.tb01075.x.

Hetzroni, E., & Tannous, J. (2004). Effects of a computer-based intervention program on the communicative functions of children with Autism. *Journal of Autism and Developmental Disorders, 34*(2), 95–113. doi:10.1023/B:JADD.0000022602.40506.bf.

Hill, E. (2004). Evaluating the theory of executive dysfunction in autism. *Developmental Review, 24*, 189–233. doi:10.1016/j.dr.2004.01.001.

Hill, E., & Frith, U. (2003). Understanding autism: Insights from mind and brain. *Philosophical Transactions of the Royal Society of London Series B: Biological Sciences, 358*, 281–289. doi:10.1098/rstb.2002.1209.

Hodgetts, S., Magill-Evans, J., & Misiaszek, J. (2011). Weighted vests, stereotyped behaviors and arousal in children with Autism. *Journal of Autism and Developmental Disorders, 41*(6), 805–814. doi:10.1007/s10803-010-1104-x.

Hoffman, C., Sweeney, D., Lopez-Wagner, M. C., Hodge, D., Nam, C. Y., & Botts, B. H. (2008). Children with Autism: Sleep problems and mothers' stress. *Focus on Autism and Other Developmental Disabilities, 23*(3), 155–165. doi:10.1177/1088357608316271.

Horner, R., Carr, E., Halle, J., McGee, G., Odom, S., Odom, M., et al. (2005). The use of single-subject research to identify evidence-based practice in special education. *Exceptional Children, 71*(2), 165–179.

Iacono, I., Lehmann, H., Marti, P., Robins, B., Dautenhahn, K. (2011). Robots as social mediators for children with Autism—A preliminary analysis comparing two different robotic platforms. *Annual International Conference of the IEEE on Development and Learning*, pp. 1–6. doi: 10.1109/DEVLRN.2011.6037322.

Ingersoll, B., & Hambrick, D. (2011). The relationship between the broader autism phenotype, child severity, and stress and depression in parents of children with Autism Spectrum Disorders. *Research in Autism Spectrum Disorders, 5*(1), 337–344. doi:10.1016/j.rasd.2010.04.017.

Iovannone, R., Dunlap, G., Huber, H., & Kincaid, D. (2003). Effective educational practices for students with autism spectrum disorders. *Focus on Autism and Other Developmental Disabilities, 18*(3), 150–165.

Ivey, J. (2004). What do parents expect? A study of likelihood and importance issues for children with autism spectrum disorders. *Focus on Autism and Other Developmental Disabilities, 19*(1), 27–33.

Jones, C., Happé, F., Golden, H., Marsden, A., Tregay, J., Simonoff, E., et al. (2009). Reading and arithmetic in adolescents with autism spectrum disorders: Peaks and dips in attainment. *Neuropsychology, 23*(6), 718–728. doi:10.1037/a0016360.

Kaminsky, L., & Dewey, D. (2001). Siblings relationships of children with Autism. *Journal of Autism and Developmental Disorders, 31*(4), 399–410. doi:10.1023/A:1010664603039.

Klin, A., Jones, W., Schultz, R., & Volkmar, F. (2003). The enactive mind, or from actions to cognition: Lessons from Autism. *Philosophical Transactions of the Royal Society of London. Series B: Biological Sciences, 358*(1430), 345–360.

Knight, V., McKissick, B., & Saunders, A. (2013). A review of technology-based interventions to teach academic skills to students with autism spectrum disorder. *Journal of Autism and Developmental Disorders, 43*(11), 2628–2648. doi:10.1007/s10803-013-1814-y.

Knott, F., Lewis, C., & Williams, T. (1995). Sibling interaction of children with learning disabilities: A comparison of autism and Down's Syndrome. *Journal of Child Psychology and Psychiatry, 36*(6), 965–976.

Koegel, R., & Wilhelm, H. (1973). Selective responding to the components of multiple visual cues by autistic children. *Journal of Experimental Child Psychology, 15*(3), 442–453.

Koegel, L., Singh, A., & Koegel, R. (2010). Improving motivation for academics in children with autism. *Journal of Autism and Developmental Disorders, 40*(9), 1057–1066.

Kumar, S., Kumar, A., & Singh, A. (2010). Understanding autism: An introduction for parents. *International Journal of Pharmacological and Biological Sciences, 1*(3), 1–13.

Lake, J., & Billingsley, B. (2000). An analysis of factors that contribute to parent-school conflict in special education. *Remedial and Special Education, 21*(4), 240–252.

Light, J., Roberts, B., Dimarco, R., & Greiner, N. (1998). Augmentative and alternative communication to support receptive and expressive communication for people with Autism. *Journal of Communication Disorders, 31*(2), 153–180. dx.doi.org/10.1016/S0021-9924(97)00087-7.

Lytle, R., & Todd, T. (2009). Stress and the student with autism spectrum disorders: Strategies for stress reduction and enhanced learning. *Teaching Exceptional Children, 41*(4), 36–42.

MacDonald, R., Clark, M., Garrigan, E., & Vangala, M. (2005). Using video modeling to teach pretend play to children with autism. *Behavioral Interventions, 20*(5), 225–238. doi:10.1002/bin.197.

Macintosh, K., & Dissanayake, C. (2006). Social skills and problem behaviours in school aged children with high-functioning autism and asperger's disorder. *Journal of Autism and Developmental Disorders, 36*(8), 1065–1076. doi:10.1007/s10803-006-0139-5.

Mancil, R. G., Todd, H., & Whitby, P. (2009). Differentiated effects of paper and computer-assisted social stories™ on inappropriate behavior in children with Autism. *Focus on Autism and Other Developmental Disabilities, 24*(4), 205–215. doi:10.1177/1088357609347324.

Mann, T. A., & Walker, P. (2003). Autism and a deficit in broadening the spread of visual attention. *Journal of Child Psychology and Psychiatry, 44*(2), 274–284.

Marshall, M. C. (2002). Asperger's syndrome: Implications for nursing practice. *Issues in Mental Health Nursing, 23*(6), 605–615. doi:10.1080/01612840290052749.

Mays, N. M., Beal-Alvarez, J., & Jolivette, K. (2011). Using movement-based sensory interventions to address self-stimulatory behaviors in students with Autism. *Teaching Exceptional Children, 43*(6), 46–52.

Mazurek, M., Wenstrup, C. (2013). Television, Video game and social media use among children with ASD and typically developing siblings. *Journal of Autism and Developmental Disorders, 43*(6), 1258–1271. doi:10.1007/s10803-012-1659-9.

McConnell, S. (2002). Interventions to facilitate social interaction for young children with autism: Review of available research and recommendations for educational intervention and future research. *Journal of Autism and Developmental Disorders, 32*(5), 351–372. doi:10.1023/A:1020537805154.

Meadan, H., Ostrosky, M., Triplett, B., Michna, A., & Fettig, A. (2011). Using visual supports with young children with autism spectrum disorder. *Teaching Exceptional Children, 43*(6), 28–35.

Meching, L., Gast, D., & Seid, N. (2009). Using a personal digital assistant to increase independent task completion by students with autism spectrum disorder. *Journal of Autism and Developmental Disabilities, 39*(10), 1420–1434. doi:10.1007/s10803-009-0761-0.

Millar, D., Light, J., & Schlosser, R. (2006). The impact of augmentative and alternative communication intervention on the speech production of individuals with developmental disabilities: A research review. *Journal of Speech, Language, and Hearing Research, 49*(2), 248–264. doi:10.1044/1092-4388(2006/021.

Mitchell, P., Parsons, S., & Leonard, A. (2007). Using virtual environements for teaching social understanding to 6 adolescents with Autistic Spectrum Disorders. *Journal of Autism and Developmental Disorders, 37*(3), 589–600. doi:10.1007/s10803-006-0189-8.

Moore, D., Cheng, Y., McGrath, P., & Powell, N. (2005). Collaborative virtual environment technology for people with autism. *Focus on Autism and Other Developmental Disabilities, 20*(4), 231–243. doi:10.1177/10883576050200040501.

Mottron, L. (2011). Nov. 3). *The power of autism. Nature, 479*, 33–35.

Müller, E., Schuler, A., & Yates, G. (2008). Social challenges and supports from the perspective of individuals with asperger syndrome and other autism spectrum disabilities. *Autism, 12*(2), 173–190. doi:10.1177/1362361307086664.

Murray, J., & Goldbart, J. (2009). Augmentative and alternative communication: A review of current issues. *Paediatrics and Child Health, 19*(10), 464–468. doi: http://dx.doi.org/10.1016/j.paed.2009.05.003.

Muskat, B. (2005). Enhancing academic, social, emotional, and behavioural functioning in children with Asperger Syndrome and Nonverbal learning Disability. In K. P. Stoddart (Ed.), *Children, youth and adults with Asperger Syndrome: Integrating multiple perspectives* (pp. 60–71). London: Jessica Kingsley.

Myers, B., Mackintosh, V., & Goin-Kochel, R. (2009). "My greatest joy and my greatest heart ache: "Parents' own words on how having a child in the Autism Spectrum has affected their lives and their families' lives. *Research in Autism Spectrum Disorders,3*(3), 670–684. doi:10.1016/j.rasd.2009.01.004.

Myles, B. S., & Simpson, R. L. (2002). Asperger syndrome: An overview of characteristics. *Focus on Autism and Other Developmental Disabilities, 17*(3), 132–137. doi:10.1177/10883 576020170030201.

Newton, D., Eren, R., & Ben-Avie, M. (2013). Visual supports for individuals with autism spectrum disorders. *Journal of Special Education Technology, 28*(2), 53–58.

Nikopoulous, C., & Keenan, M. (2007). Using video modeling to teach complex social sequences to children with autism. *Journal of Autism and Developmental Disorders, 37*(4), 678–693. doi:10.1007/s10803-006-0195-x.

Oberleitner, R., Ball, J., Gillette, D., Naseef, R., & Stamm, B. (2006). Technologies to lessen the distress of Autism. *Journal of Aggression, Maltreatment & Trauma, 12*(1-2), 221–242. doi:10.1300/J146v12n01_12.

Oberleitner, R., Elison-Bowers, P., Reischl, U., & Ball, J. (2007). Optimizing the personal health record with special video capture for the treatment of Autism. *Journal of Developmental and Physical Disabilities, 19*(5), 513–518. doi:10.1007/s10882-007-9067-3.

Odom, S., Brown, W., Frey, T., Karasu, N., Smith-Canter, L., & Strain, P. (2003). Evidence-based practices for young children with autism: Contributions for single-subject design research. *Focus on Autism and Other Developmental Disabilities, 18*(3), 166–175. doi:10.1177/10883 576030180030401.

Offit, P. (2007). Thimerosal and vaccines—A cautionary tale. *The New England Journal of Medicine. 357*, 1278–1279. Retrieved from http://www.nejm.org.

Panyan, M. (1984). Computer technology for autistic students. *Journal of Autism and Developmental Disorders, 14*(4), 375–382.

Panyan, M., McGregor, G., Bennett, A., Rysticken, N., & Spurr, A. (1984, January). The effects of microcomputer based instruction on the academic and social progress of autistic students. Paper presented at the Council for Exceptional Children Technology in Special Education Conference, Reno, Nevada.

Parker, S., Schwartz, B., Todd, J., & Pickering, L. (2004). Thimerosal-containing vaccines and Autistic Spectrum Disorder: A critical review of published original data. *Pediatrics, 114*, 793–796. Retrieved from http://www.pediatrics.org/cgi/content/full/114/3/793.

Parsons, S., Leonard, A., & Mitchell, P. (2006). Virtual environments for social skills training: Comments from two adolescents with autistic spectrum disorder. *Computers and Education, 47*(2), 186–206. doi:10.1016/j.compedu.2004.10.003.

Parsons, S., & Mitchell, P. (2002). The potential of virtual reality in social skills training for people with autistic spectrum disorders. *Journal of Intellectual Disability Research, 46*(5), 430–443. doi:10.1046/j.1365-2788.2002.00425.x.

Parsons, S., Newbutt, N., & Wallace, S. (2014). Using virtual reality technology to support the learning of children on the autism spectrum. In K. Boser, M. Goodwin, & S. Wayland (Eds.), *Technology tools for students with autism* (pp. 63–84). Baltimore, MD: Paul H. Brookes Publishing Co.

Parsons, T., Rizzo, A., Rogers, S., & York, P. (2009). Virtual reality in paediatric rehabilitation: A review. *Developmental Neurorehabilitation, 12*(4), 224–238. doi:10.1080/17518420902991719.

Pellicano, E., Maybery, M., Durkin, K., & Maley, A. (2006). Multiple cognitive capabilities/deficits in children with an autism spectrum disorder: "Weak" central coherence and its relationship to theory of mind and executive control. *Development and Psychopathology, 18*(1), 77–98. doi:10.1017/S0954579406060056.

Pennington, R. (2010). Computer-Assisted Instruction for teaching academic skills to students with autism spectrum disorders: A review of literature. *Focus on Autism and Other Developmental Disabilities, 25*(4), 239–248. doi:10.1177/1088357610378291.

Perreault, A., Gurnsey, R., Dawson, M., Mottron, L., & Bertone, A. (2011). Increased sensitivity to mirror symmetry in autism. *PLoS ONE,6*(4), e19519. doi:10.1371/journal.pone.0019519.

Pleinis, A., & Romanczyk, R. (1983, May). Computer assisted instruction for atypical children: Attention, performance, and collateral behavior. Paper presented at the Applied Behavior Analysis Conference, Milwaukee.

Ploog, B. O., Scharf, A., Nelson, D., & Brooks, P. J. (2013). Use of computer-assisted technologies (CAT) to enchance social, communicative, and language development in children with autism spectrum disorders. *Journal of Autism and Developmental Disorders, 43*(2), 301–322. doi:10.1007/s10803-012-1571-3.

Portway, S., & Johnson, B. (2005). Do you know I have asperger's syndrome? Risks of a non-obvious disability. *Health, Risk & Society, 7*(1), 73–83. doi:10.1080/09500830500042086.

Premack, D., & Woodruff, G. (1978). Does the chimpanzee have a theory of mind? *Behavioral and Brain Sciences, 1*, 515–526.

Prizant, B.M., & Rydell, P. (1984). Analysis of functions of delayed echolalia in Autistic Children. Retrieved March 8, 2014 from: http://www.barryprizant.com/files/functions_de_19 84.pdf.

Quill, K. (1997). Instructional considerations for young children with autism: The rationale for visually cued instruction. *Journal of Autism and Developmental Disorders, 27*(6), 697–714.

Rajendan, G., & Mitchell, P. (2007). Cognitive theories of Autism. *Developmental Review, 27*(2), 224–260. doi:10.1016/j.dr.2007.02.001.

Rapin, I., & Dunn, M. (1997). Language disorders in children with Autism. *Seminars in Pediatric Neurology, 4*(2), 86–92. doi:10.1016/S071-9091(97)80024-1.

Rayner, G. (2005). Meeting the educational needs of the student with Asperger Syndrome through assessment, advocacy, and accommodations. In K. P. Stoddart (Ed.), *Children, youth and adults with asperger syndrome: Integrating multiple perspectives* (pp. 184–196). Philadelphia, PA: Jessica Kingsley Publishers.

Reynolds, B., Newsom, C., & Lovaas, O. (1974). Auditory overselectivity in autistic children. *Journal of Abnormal Child Psychology, 2*(4), 253–263. doi:10.1007/BF00919253.

Riva, G., & Gamberini, L. (2001). 7 Virtual Reality in telemedicine. In G. Riva and F. Davide (Eds.), *Communications Through Virtual Technology: Identity Community and Technology in the Internet Age* (pp. 101–117). Retrieved from http://www.neurovr.org/emerging/book1/1CHAPT_07.PDF.

Rivers, J., & Stoneman, Z. (2003). Sibling relationships when a child has Autism: Marital stress and support coping. *Journal of Autism and Developmental Disorders, 33*(4), 383–394. doi:10.1023/A:1025006727395.

Robins, B., Dautenhahn, K., Boekhorst, T., & Billard, A. (2005). Robotic assistants in therapy and education of children with autism: Can a small humanoid robot help encourage social interaction skills? *Universal Access in the Information Society, 4*(2), 105–120. doi:10.1007/s10209-005-0116-3.

Roblyer, M. D., & Doering, A. H. (2010). *Integrating Educational Technology into Teaching* (5th ed.). Boston, MA: Allyn & Bacon.

Roeyers, H., & Mycke, K. (1995). Siblings of children with autism, with mental retardation and with normal development. *Child: Care, Health, & Development, 21*(5), 305–319. doi:10.1111/j.1365-2214.1995.tb00760.x.

Romanczyk, R., & Gillis, J. (2005). Treatment approaches for autism: Evaluating options and making informed choices. In D. Zager (Ed.), *Autism spectrum disorders identification, education, and treatment* (3rd ed., pp. 515–535). Mahwah, NJ: Lawrence Erlbaum Associates.

Samson, F., Mottron, L., Souliéres, I., & Zeffiro, T. (2011). Exceptional visual abilities explained. *ScienceDaily*. Retrieved December 4, 2013, from http://www.sciencedaily.com/releases/2011/04/110404093149.htm.

References

Scattone, D., Wilczynski, S., Edwards, R., & Rabian, B. (2002). Decreasing disruptive behaviors of children with autism using social stories. *Journal of Autism and Developmental Disorders, 32*(6), 535–543. doi:10.1023/A:1021250813367.

Schreibman, L. (2005). *The science and fiction of autism.* Cambridge: Harvard University Press.

Schwichtenberg, A., & Poehlmann, J. (2007). Applied behavior analysis: Does intervention intensity relate to family stressors and maternal well-being? *Journal of Intellectual Disability Research, 51*(8), 598–605. doi:10.1111/j.1365-2788.2006.00940.x.

Scott, J., & Baldwin, W. (2005). Definitions and characteristics of the Spectrum. In D. Zager (Ed.), *Autism spectrum disorders identification, education, and treatment* (3rd ed., pp. 173–228). Mahwah, NJ: Lawrence Erlbaum Associates.

Shah, A., & Frith, U. (1993). Why do autistic individuals show superior performance on the block design task? *Journal of Child Psychology and Psychiatry, 34*(8), 1351–1364. doi:10.1111/1469-7610.ep11358375.

Shane, H., Laubscher, E., Schlosser, R., Flynn, S., Sorce, J., & Abramson, J. (2012). Applying technology to visually support language and communication in individuals with autism spectrum disorders. *Journal of Autism and Developmental Disorders, 42*(6), 1228–1235. doi:10.1007/s10803-011-1304-z.

Silva, L., & Schalock, M. (2012). Autism Parenting Stress Index: Initial psychometic evidence. *Journal of Autism and Developmental Disorders, 42*(4), 566–574. doi:10.1007/s10803-011-1274-1.

Simonoff, E., Pickles, A., Charman, T., Chandler, S., Loucas, T., & Baird, G. (2008). Psychiaric disorders in children with autism spectrum disorders: Prevalence, comorbidity, and associated factors in a population-derived sample. *Journal of the American Academy of Child and Adolescent Psychiatry, 47*(8), 921–929. doi:10.1097/CHI.0b013e318179964f.

Simpson, R. (2005). Evidence-based practices and students with autism spectrum disorders. *Focus on Autism and Other Developmental Disabilities, 20*(3), 140–149. doi:10.1177/10883576050200030201.

South, M., Ozonoff, S., & Mcmahon, W. (2007). The relationship between executive functioning, central coherence, and repetitive behaviors in the high-functioning autism spectrum. *Autism, 11*(5), 437–451. doi:10.1177/1362361307079606.

Stevenson, J., & Gernsbacher, M. (2013). Abstract spatial reasoning as an autistic strength. *PLoS ONE, 8*(3), 1–9. doi:10.1371/journal.pone.0059329.

Stoner, J., Bock, S., Thompson, J., Agell, M., Heyl, B., & Crowley, P. (2005). Welcome to our world: Parent perceptions of interactions between parents of young children with ASD and education professionals. *Focus on Autism and Other Developmental Disabilities, 20*(1), 39–51. doi:10.1177/108835760832997.

Tartaro, A., & Ratz, C. (2014). Incorporating technology into peer social group programs. In K. Boser, M. Goodwin, & S. Wayland (Eds.), *Technology tools for students with autism* (pp. 185–200). Baltimore, MD: Paul H. Brookes Publishing Co.

Tincani, M., & Boutot, E. (2005). Technology and autism: Current practices and future directions. In D. Edyburn, K. Higgins, & R. Boone (Eds.), *Handbook of special education technology research and practice.* (pp. 413–421). White Bay, WI: Knowledge by Design.

The Alan Mason Chesney Medical Archives of the Johns Hopkins Medical Institutions. (2009). Leo Kanner Collection. Retrieved from http://www.medicalarchives.jhmi.edu/papers.kanner.html.

Tobing, L., & Glenwick, D. (2007). Relations of the childhood autism rating scale-parent version to diagnosis, stress, and age. *Research in Developmental Disabilities, 23*(3), 211–223. doi:10.1016/S0891-4222(02)00099-9.

Tsai, L. (2005). Medical treatment in autism. In D. Zager (Ed.), *Autism spectrum disorders identification, education, and treatment* (3rd ed., pp. 395–492). New Jersey: Lawrence Erlbaum Associates.

Turnbull, A., & Turnbull, H. (2001). *Families, professionals, and exceptionality: Collaborating for empowerment.* OH: Merrill Prentice Hall.

Wainer, A. L., & Ingersoll, B.R. (2011). The use of innovative computer technology for teaching social communication to individuals with Autism Spectrum Disorders. Research in Autism Spectrum Disorders, 5(1), 96–107. Retrieved March 8, 2014 from http://www.editlib.org/p/106602.

Wainer, J., Ferrari, E., Dautenhahn, K., & Robins, B. (2010). The effectiveness of using a robotics class to foster collaboration among groups of children with autism in an exploratory study. *Personal and Ubiquitous Computing, 14*(5), 445–455. doi:10.1007/s00779-009-0266-z.

Weiss, M. (2013). Behavior Analytic Interventions for developing social skills in individuals with Autism. In P. Gerhardt & D. Crimmins (Eds.), *Social Skills and Adaptive Behavior in Learners with Autism Spectrum Disorders.* (pp. 33–51). Baltimore, MD: Paul H. Brookes Publishing Co.

Whalon, K., Al Otaiba, S., & Delano, M. (2009). Evidence-based reading instruction for individuals with Autism Spectrum Disorders. *Focus on autism and other developmental disabilities, 24*(1), 3–16. doi:10.1177/1088357608328515.

Whalon, K., & Hart, J. (2011). Adapting an evidence-based reading comprehension strategy for learners with Autism Spectrum Disorder. *Intervention in School and Clinic, 46*(4), 195–203. doi:10.1177/1053451210389036.

White, S. (2013). The triple I hypothesis: Taking another ('s) perspective on Executive Dysfunction in Autism. *Journal of Autism and Developmental Disorders, 43*(9), 114–121. doi:10.1007/s10803-012-1550-8.

Whyatt, C., & Craig, C. (2012). Motor skills in children aged 7–10 years, diagnosed with autism spectrum disorder. *Journal of Autism and Developmental Disorders, 42*(9), 1799–1809. doi:10.1007/s10803-011-1421-8.

Williams, D., Goldstein, G., & Minshew, N. (2006). The profile of memory function in children with Autism. *Neuropsychology, 20*(1), 21–29. doi:10.1037/0894-4105.20.1.21.

Yuen, T., Mason, L., & Gomez, A. (2014). Collaborative robotics projects for adolescents with autism spectrum disorders. *Journal of Special Education Technology, 29*(1), 51–62.

Zager, D., & Shamow, N. (2005). Teaching students with Autism Spectrum Disorders. In D. Zager (Ed.), Autism Spectrum Disorders Identification, Education, & Treatment, (3rd ed.; pp. 295–326). Mahwah, NJ: Lawrence Erlbaum Associates.

Index

A
Academics, 41, 45, 50, 58
Augmentative andalternative communication (AAC), 59, 60, 66, 67
Autism spectrum disorders (ASD), 15–18, 20–25, 30–38

C
Computerized tools, 79

I
Instructional environments, 76

L
Learners, 16, 25
Learning, 41, 49, 52, 53, 58

P
Parents, 30–34, 36, 38

R
Robotics, 59, 60, 67–69

S
Support, 15, 20, 21, 24, 26
Supporting students with ASD, 6, 9
Supports needed in ASD, 73, 75

T
Technology, 2, 13, 37–39
Technology use, 57, 58
Telepractice/teletherapy, 59, 61, 70
Theories in ASD, 2, 3

V
Video games, 59, 61, 62, 71
Video-modeling, 59, 62
Virtual reality, 59, 60, 69
Visual support, 41, 57